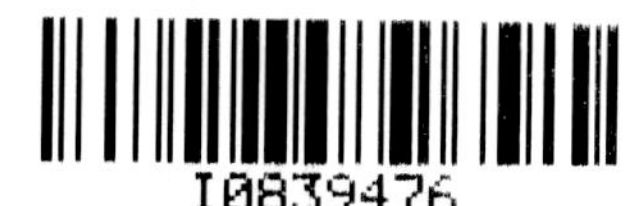

Flower Life
Coloring Book

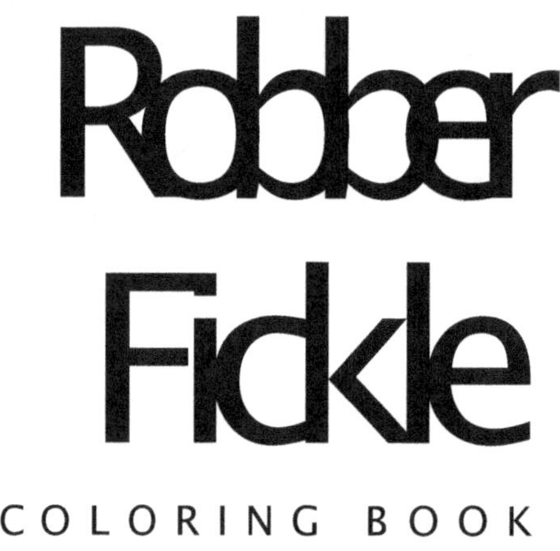

**For Any Question and Suggestions
robberfickle@gmail.com**

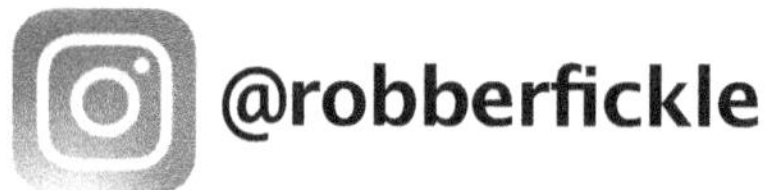

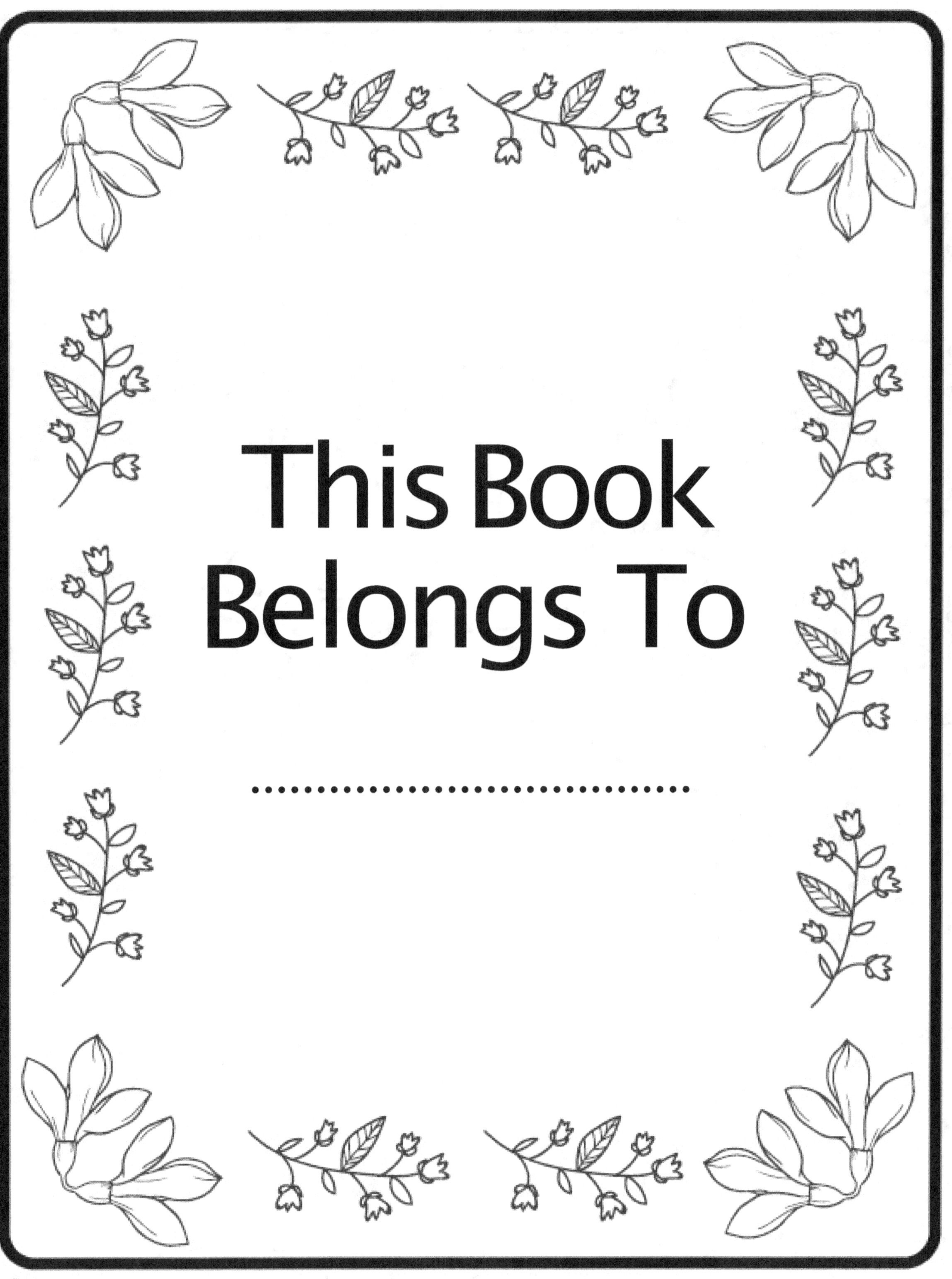

This Book
Belongs To

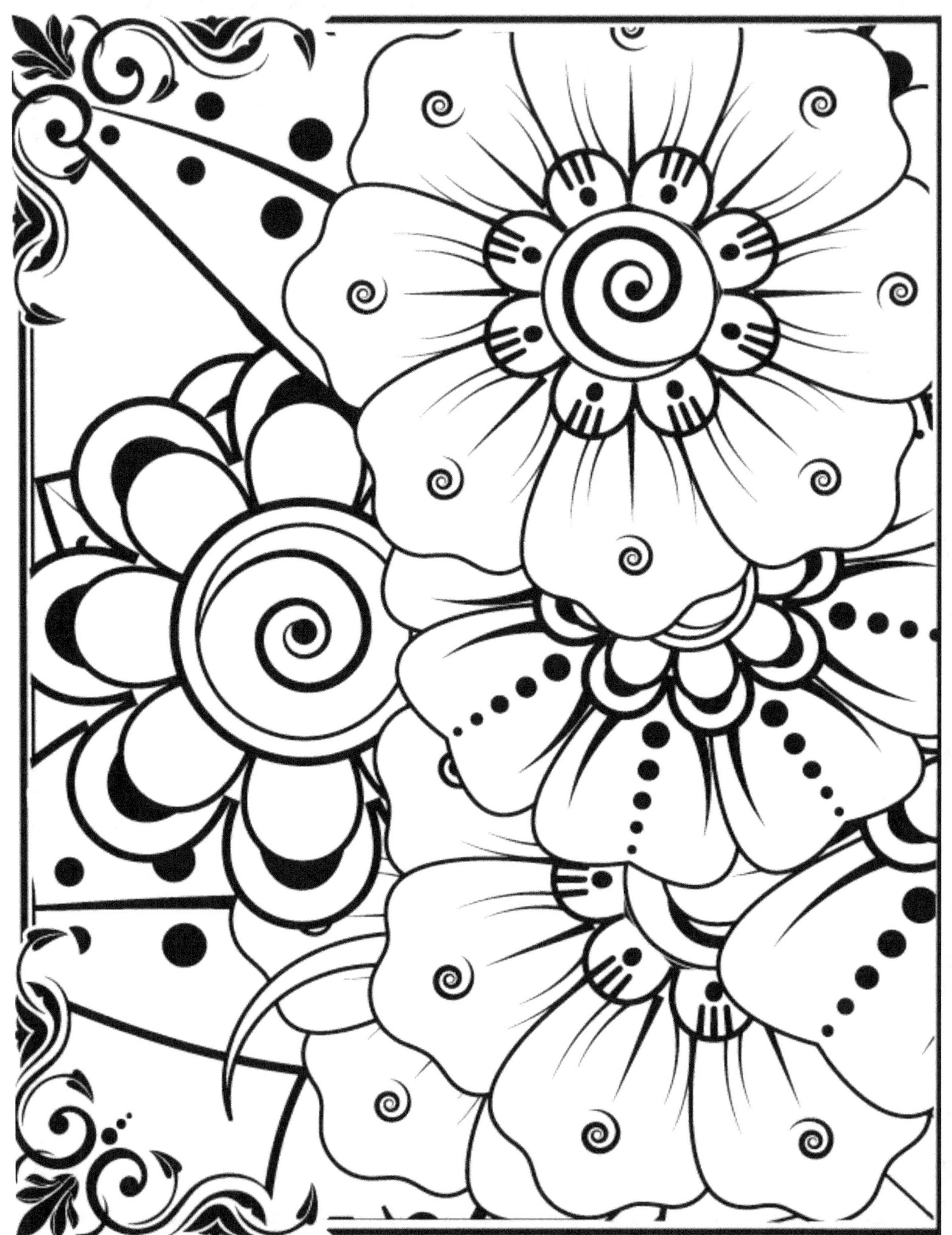

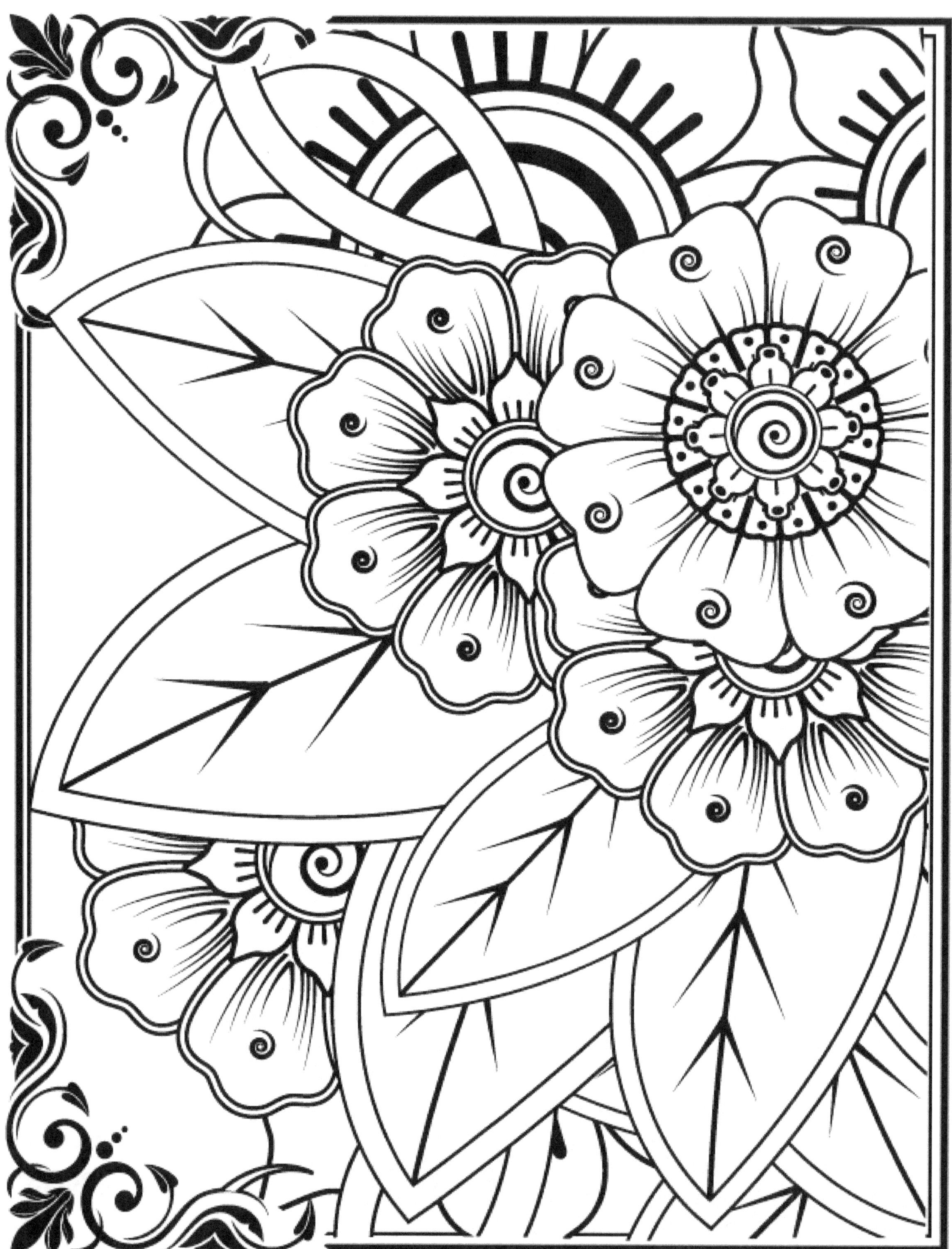

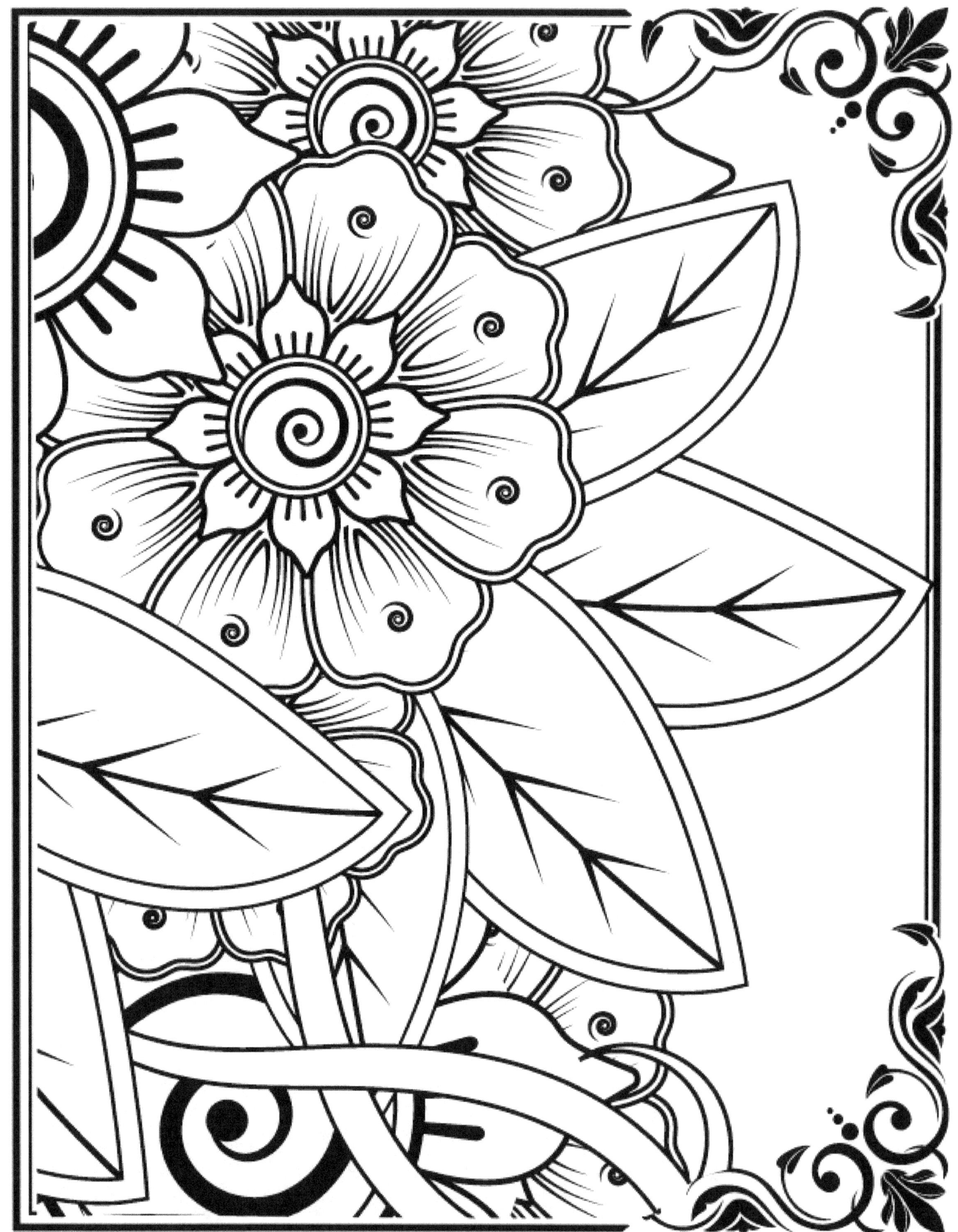

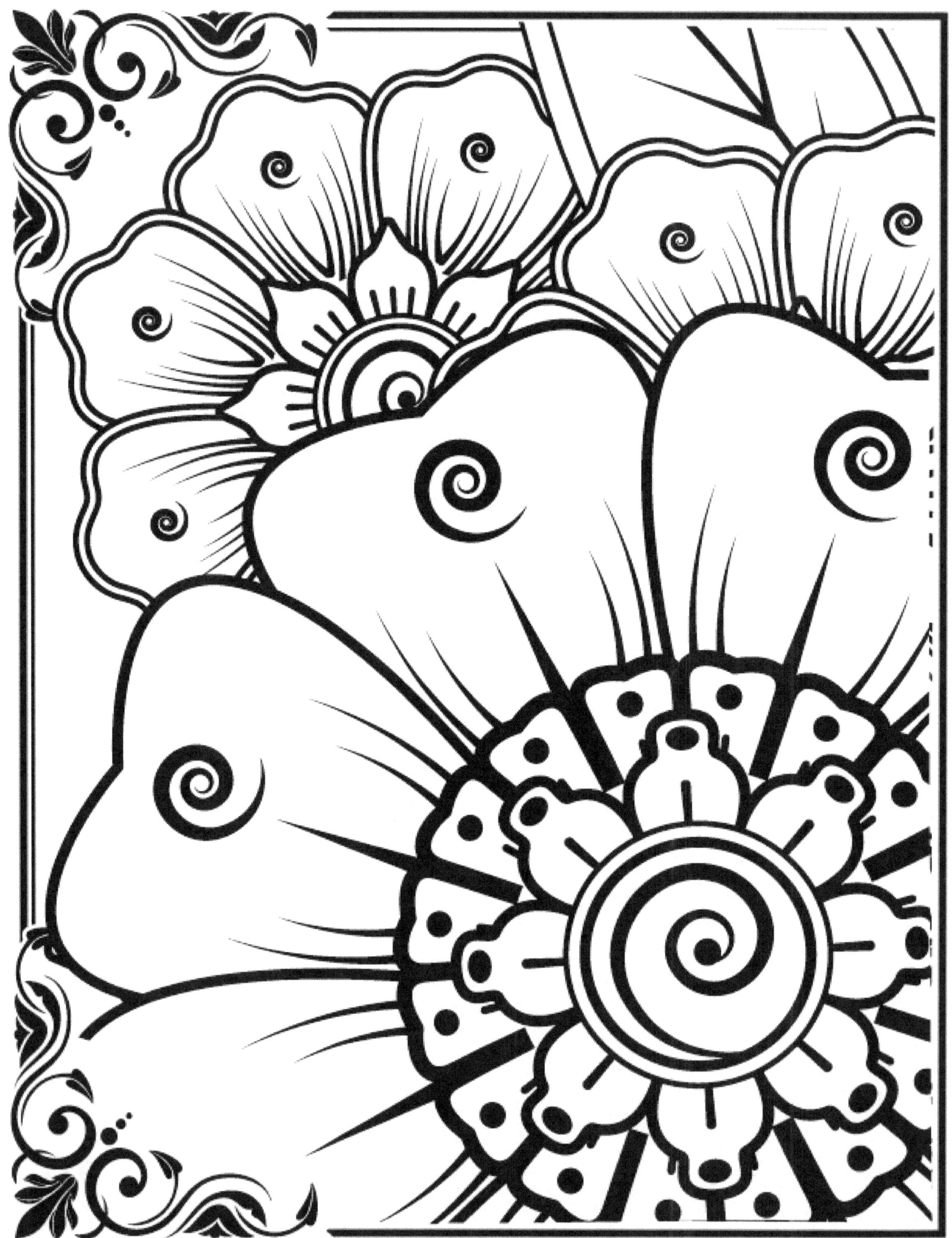

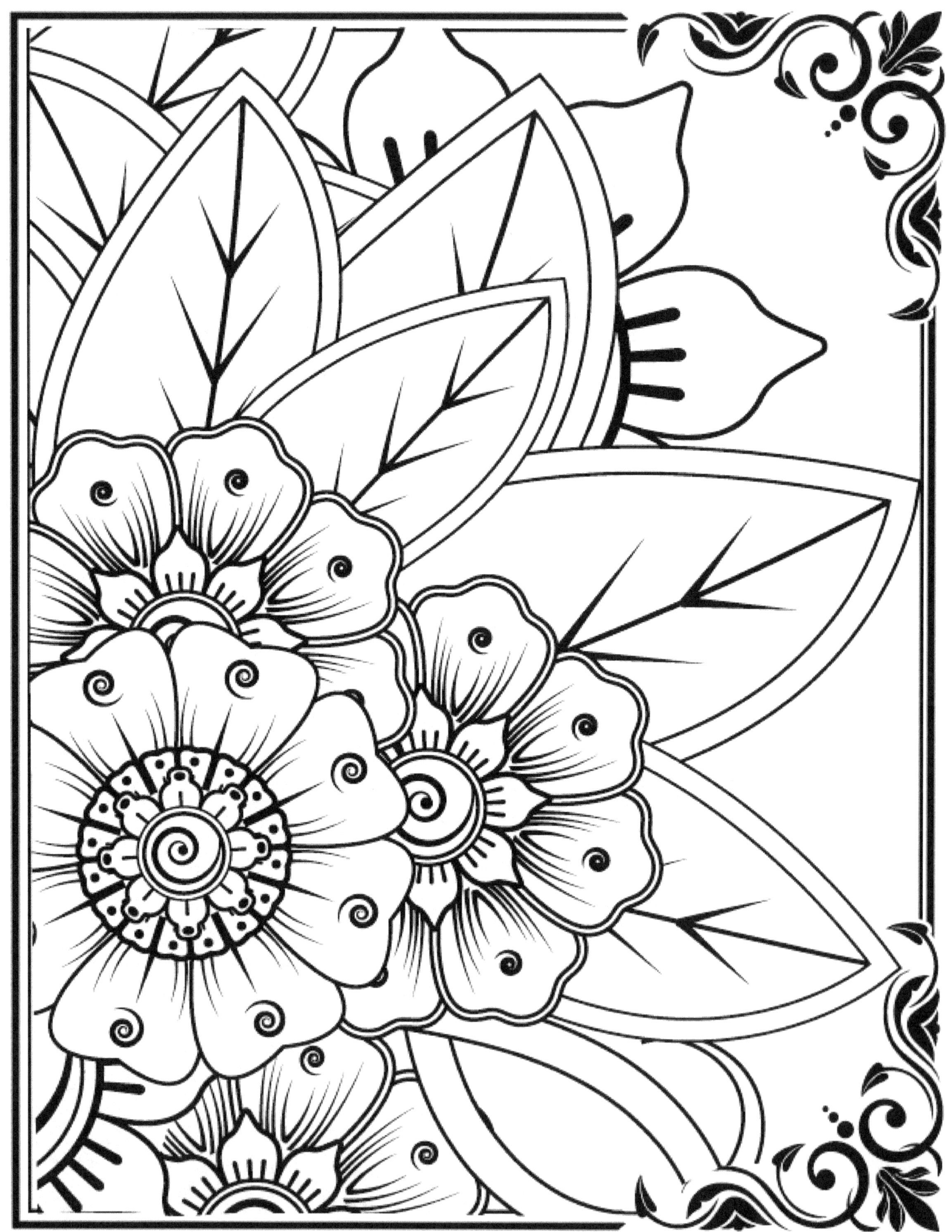

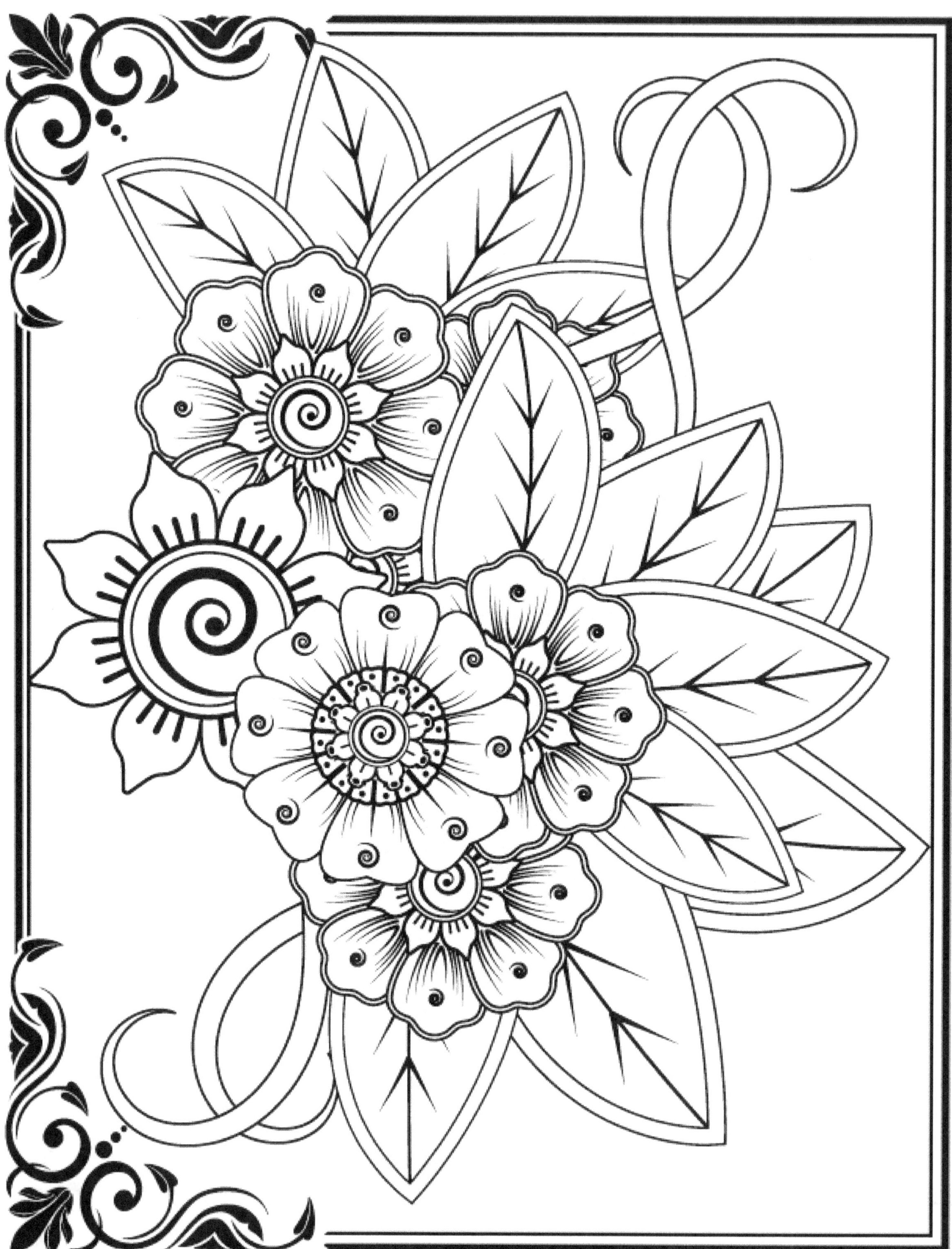

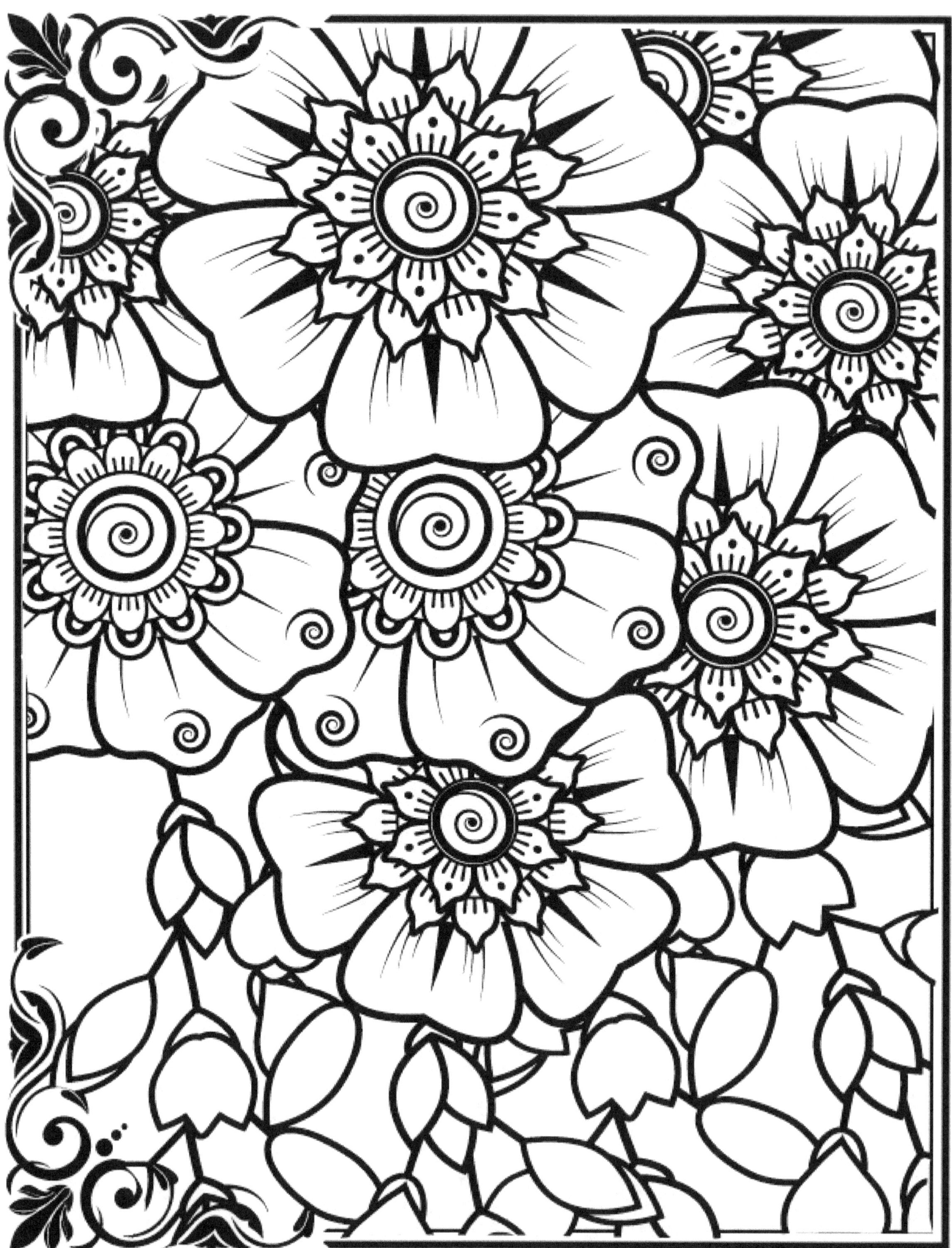

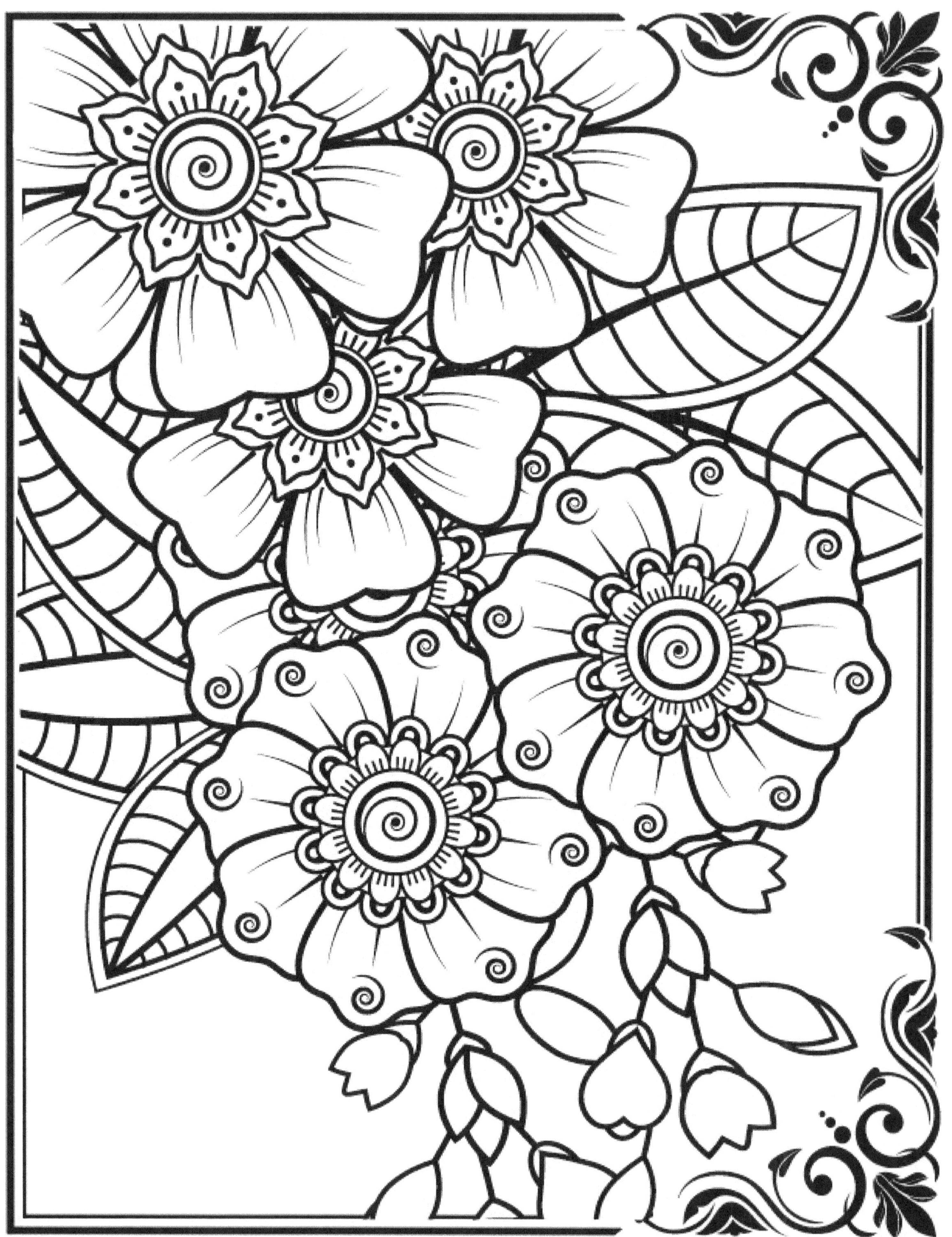

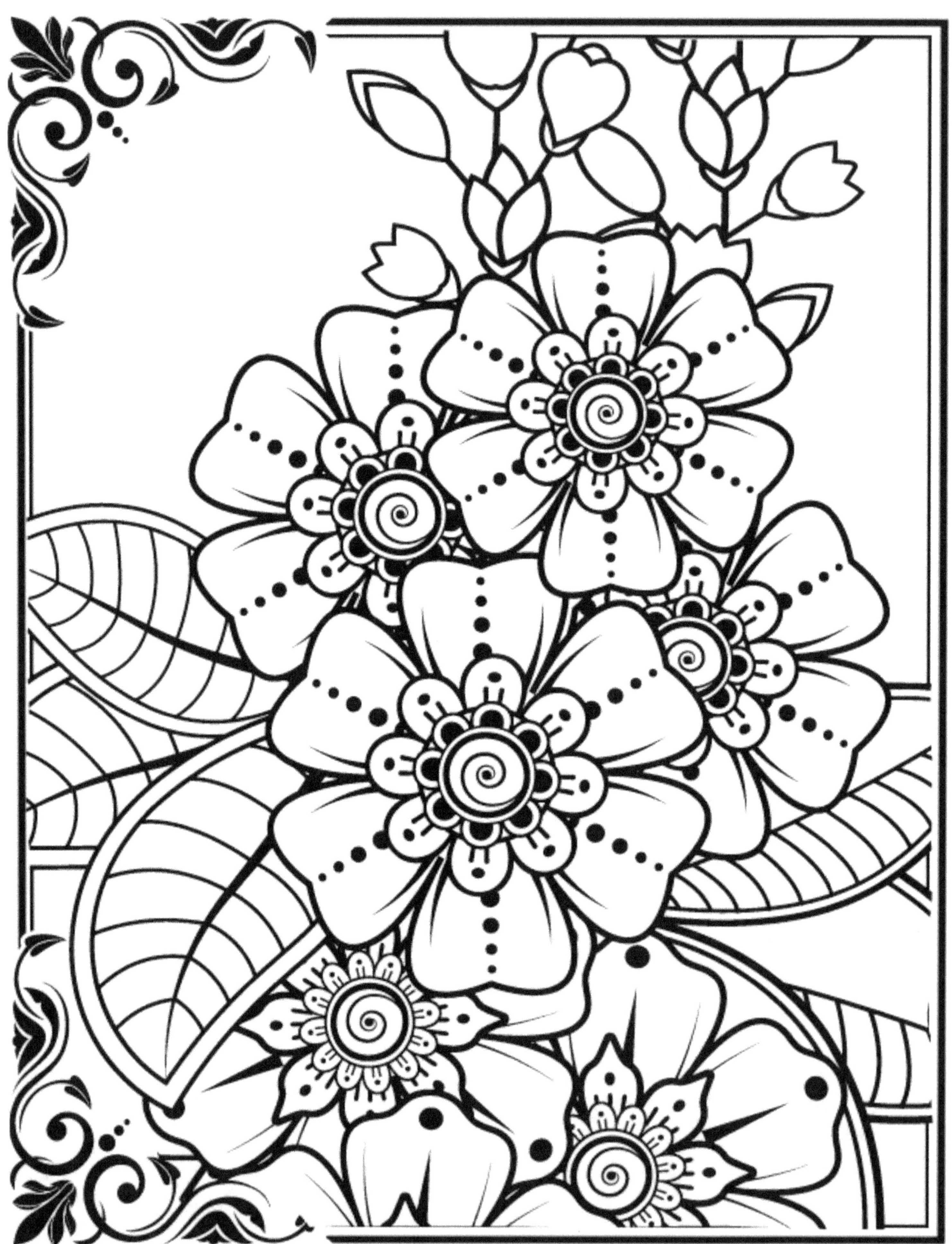

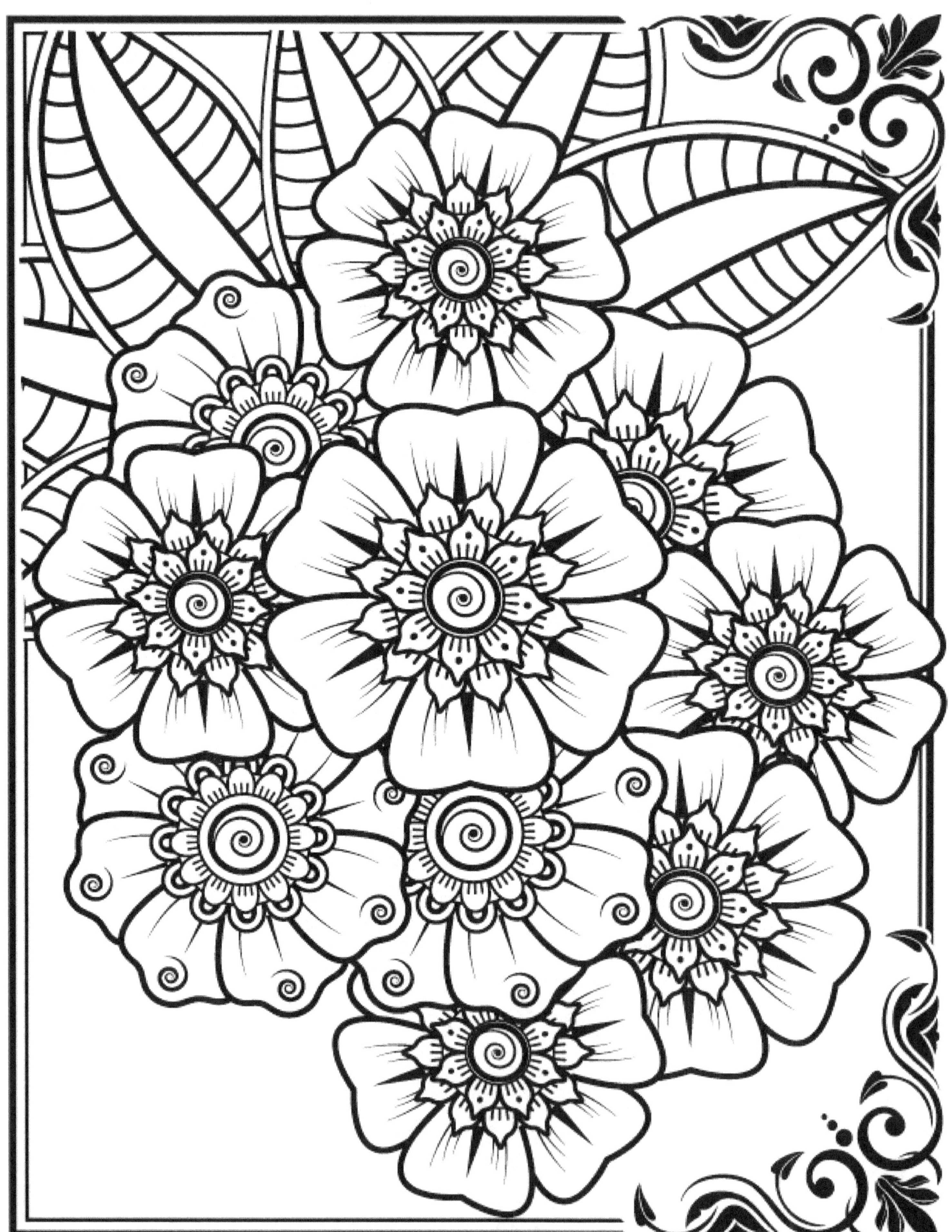

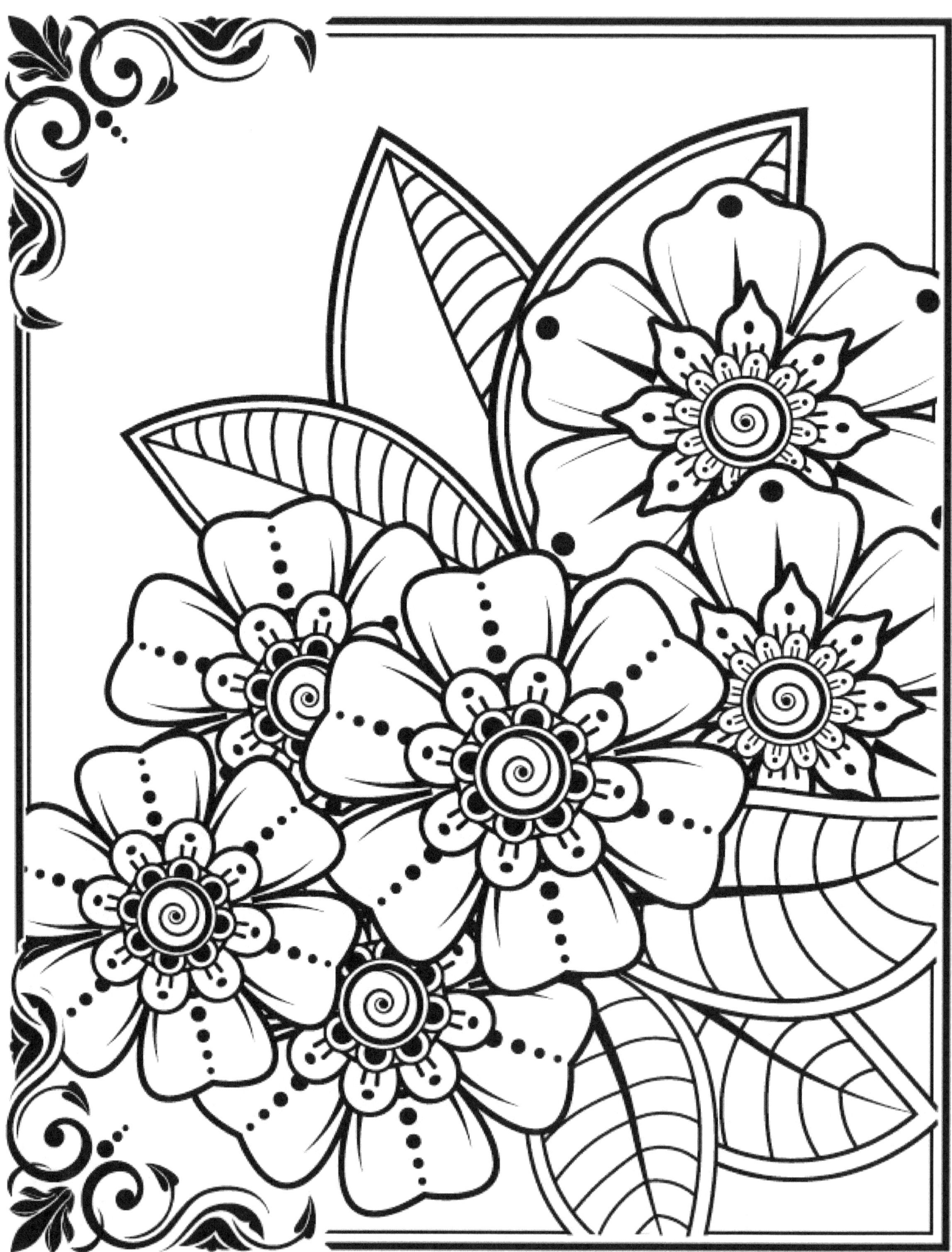

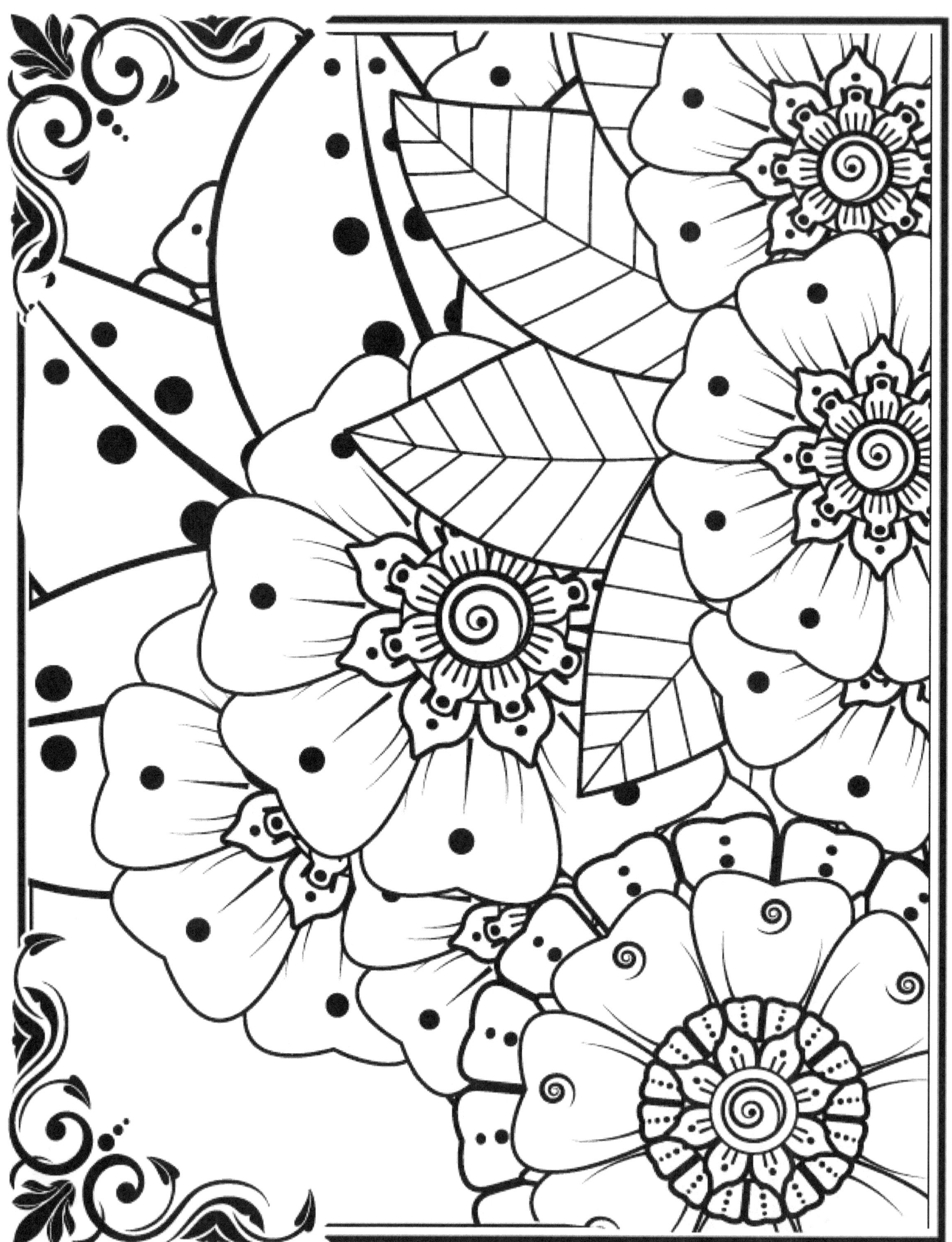

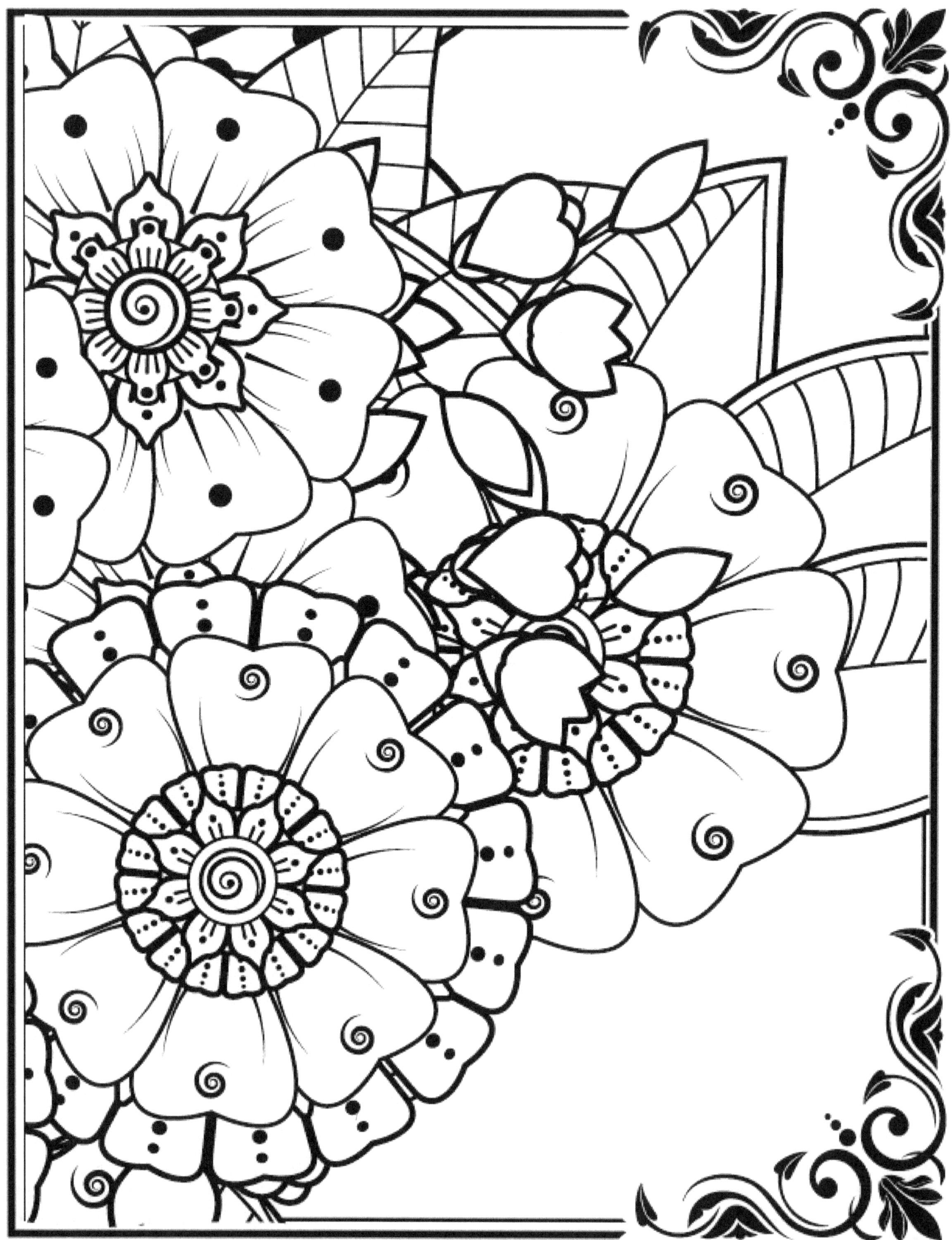

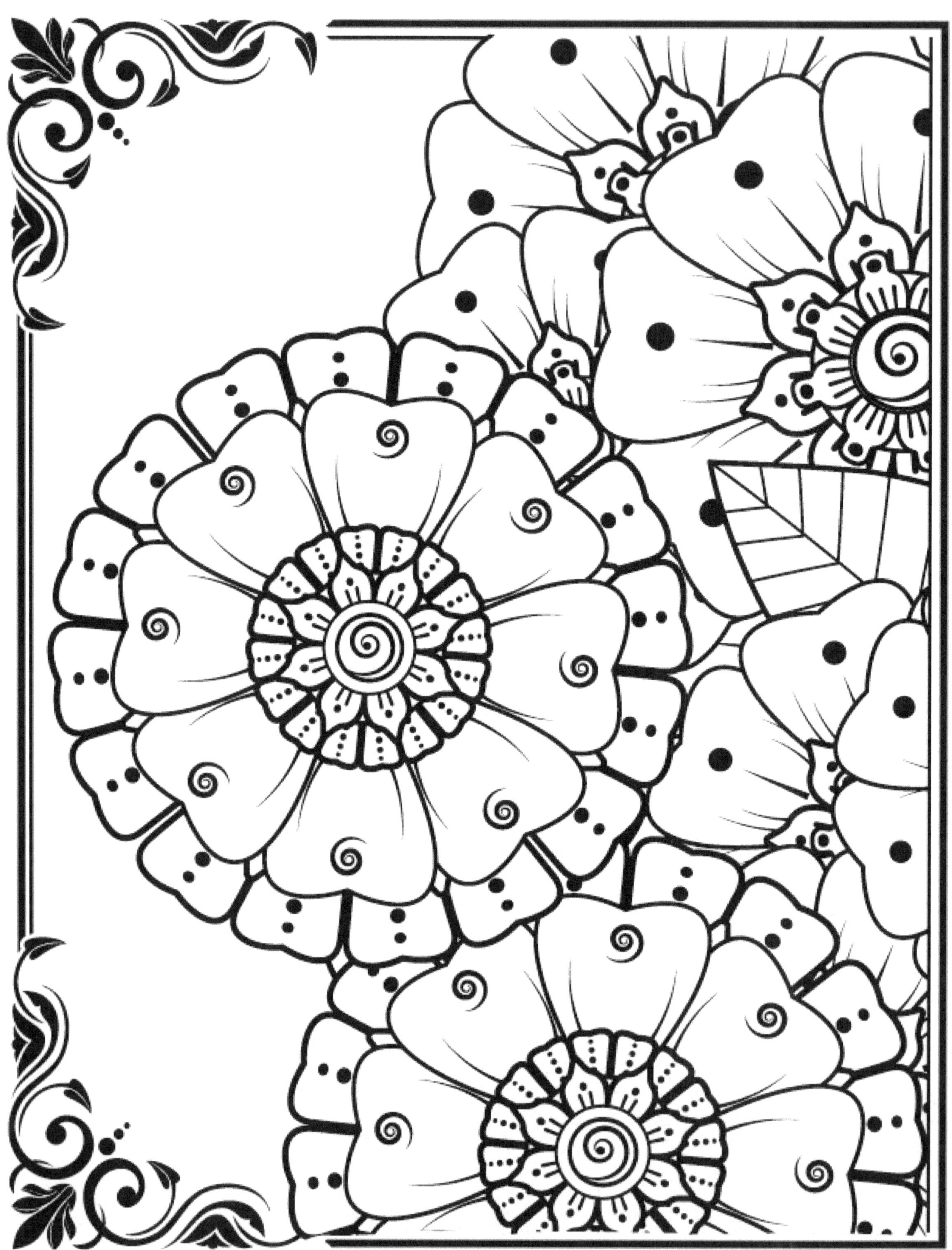

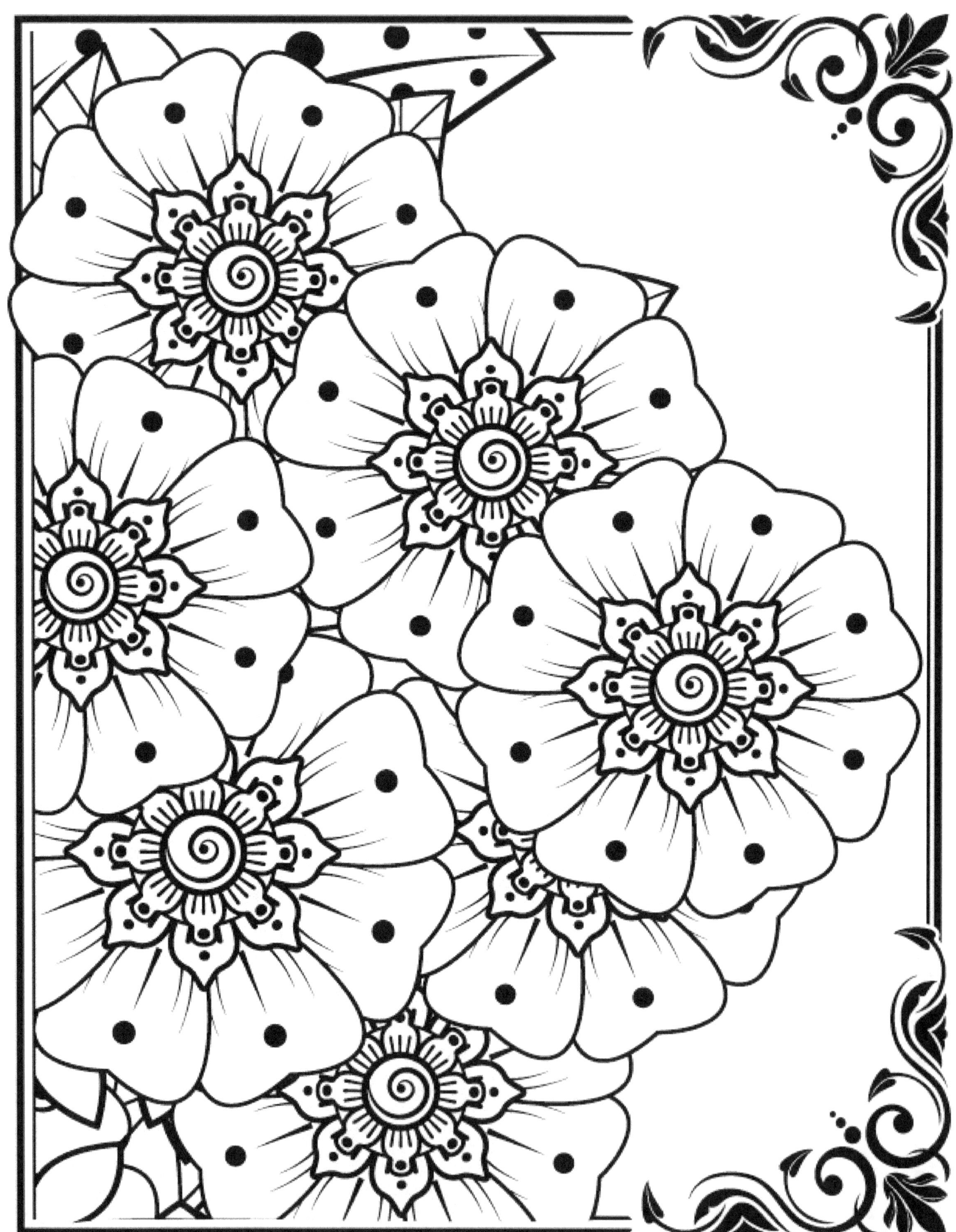

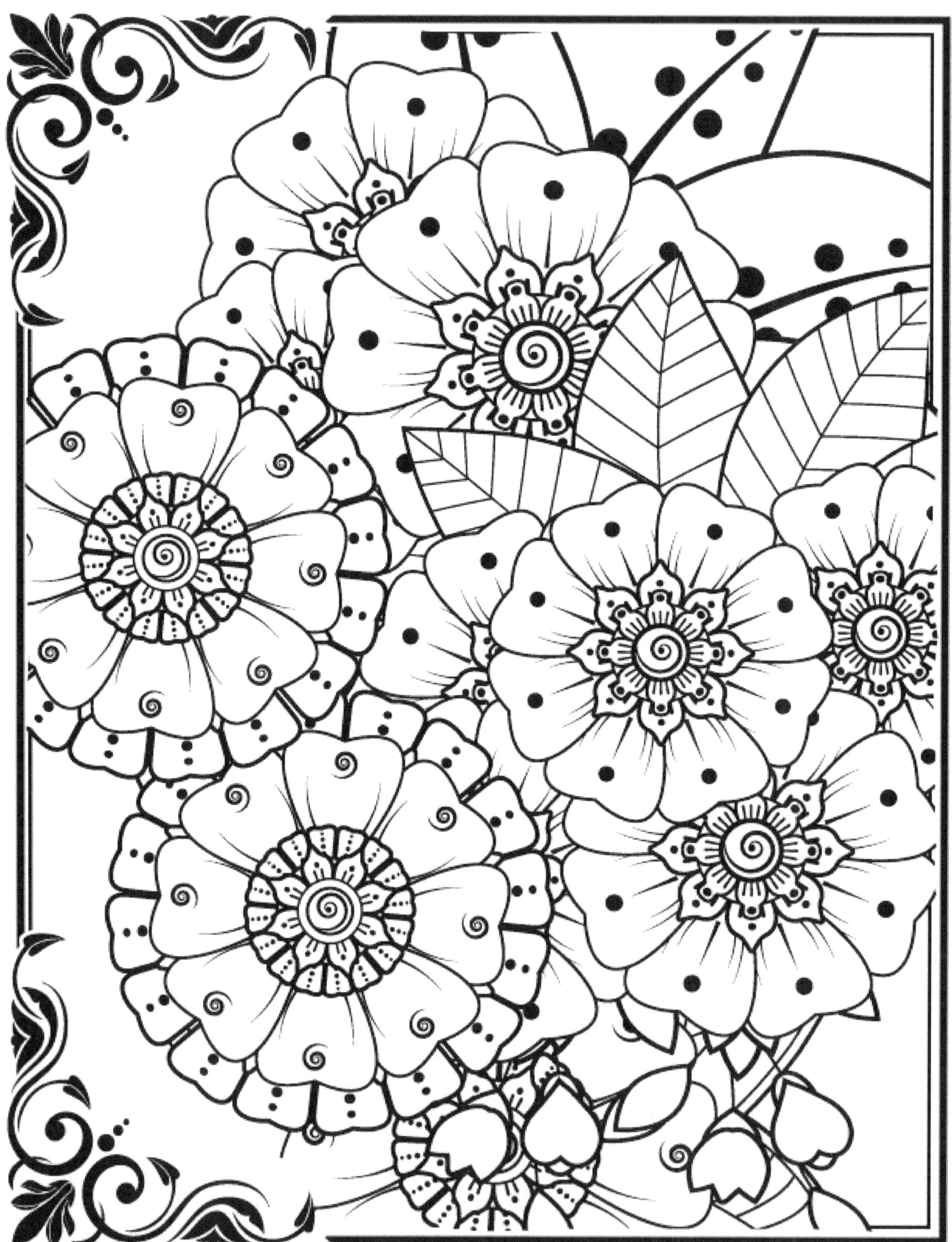

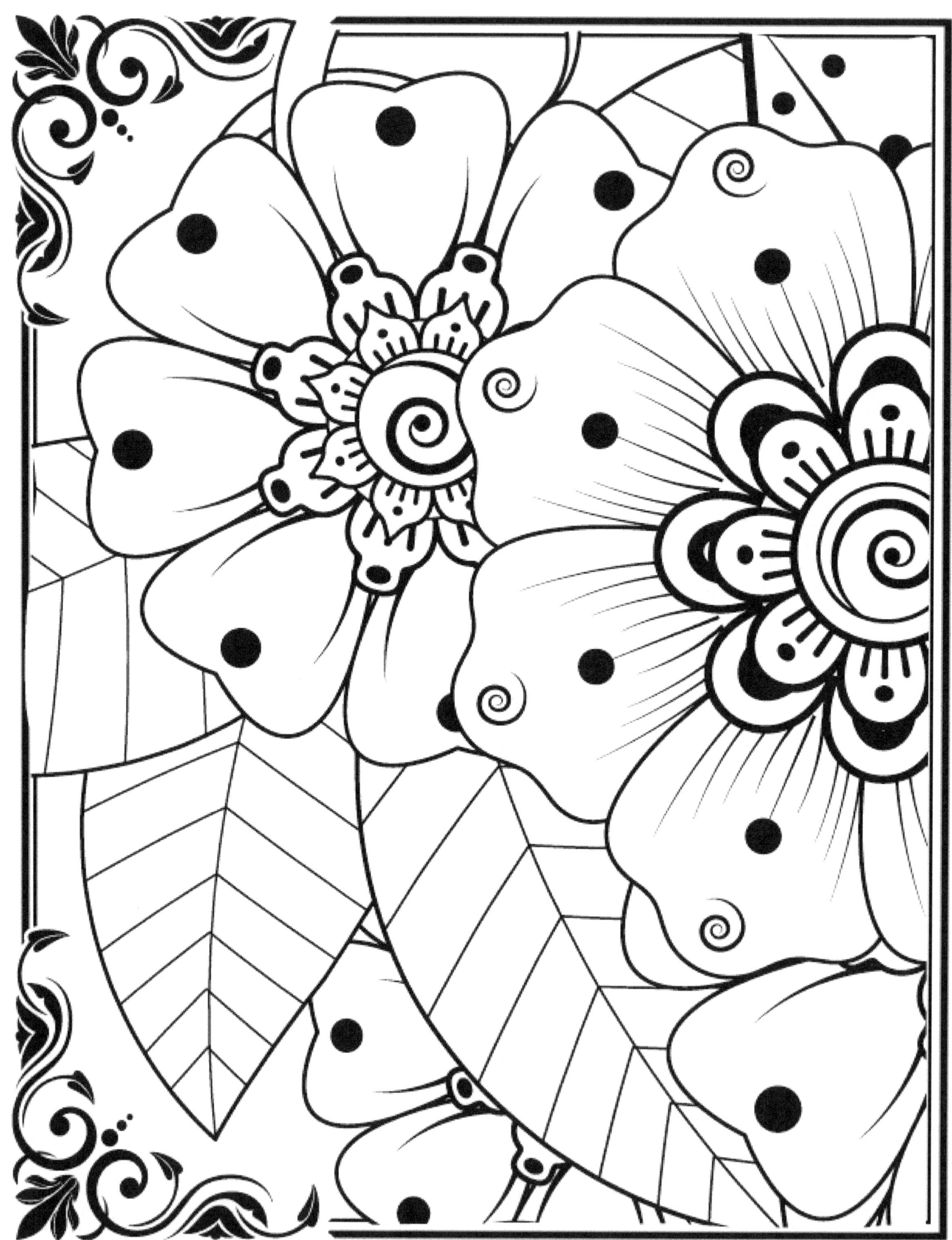

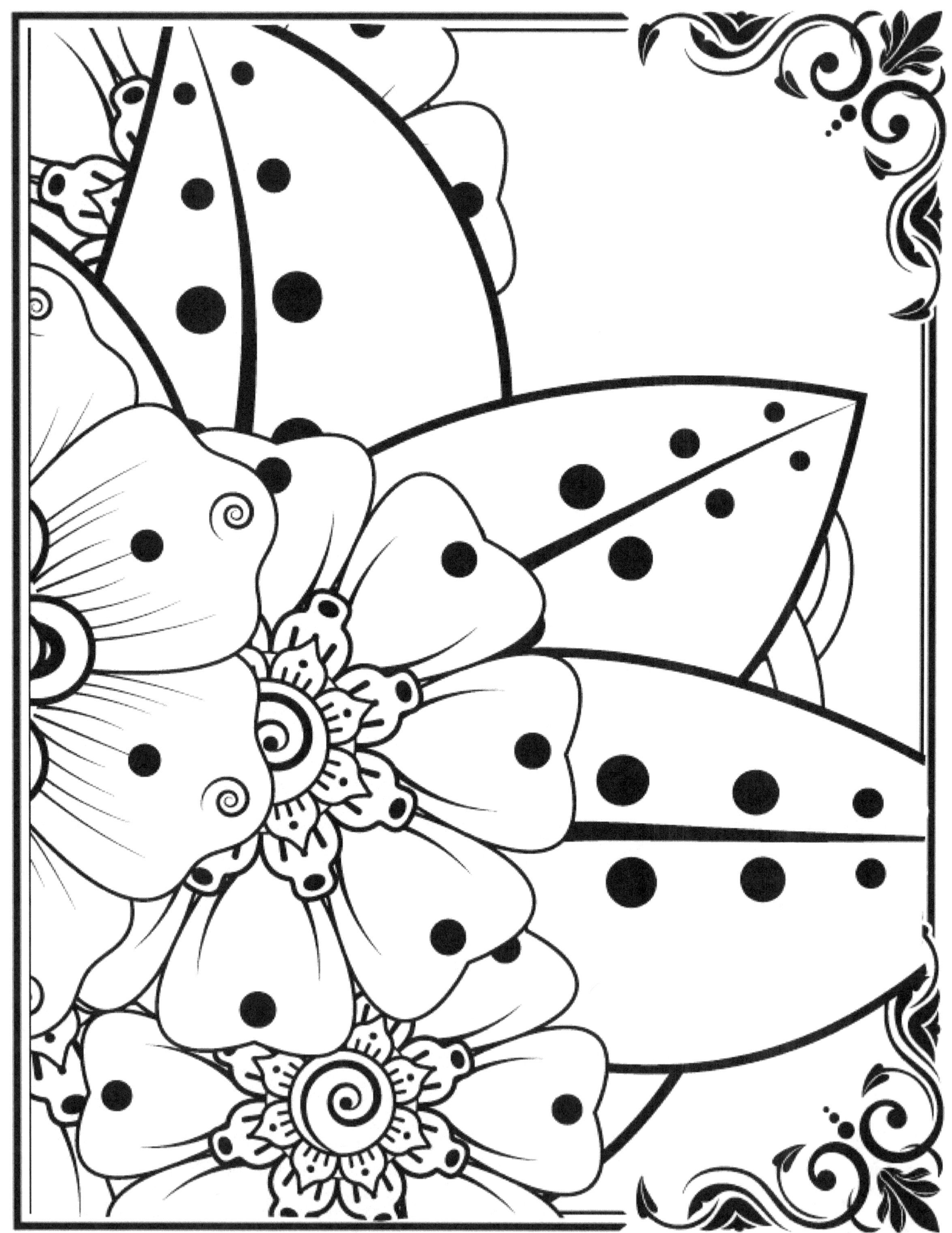

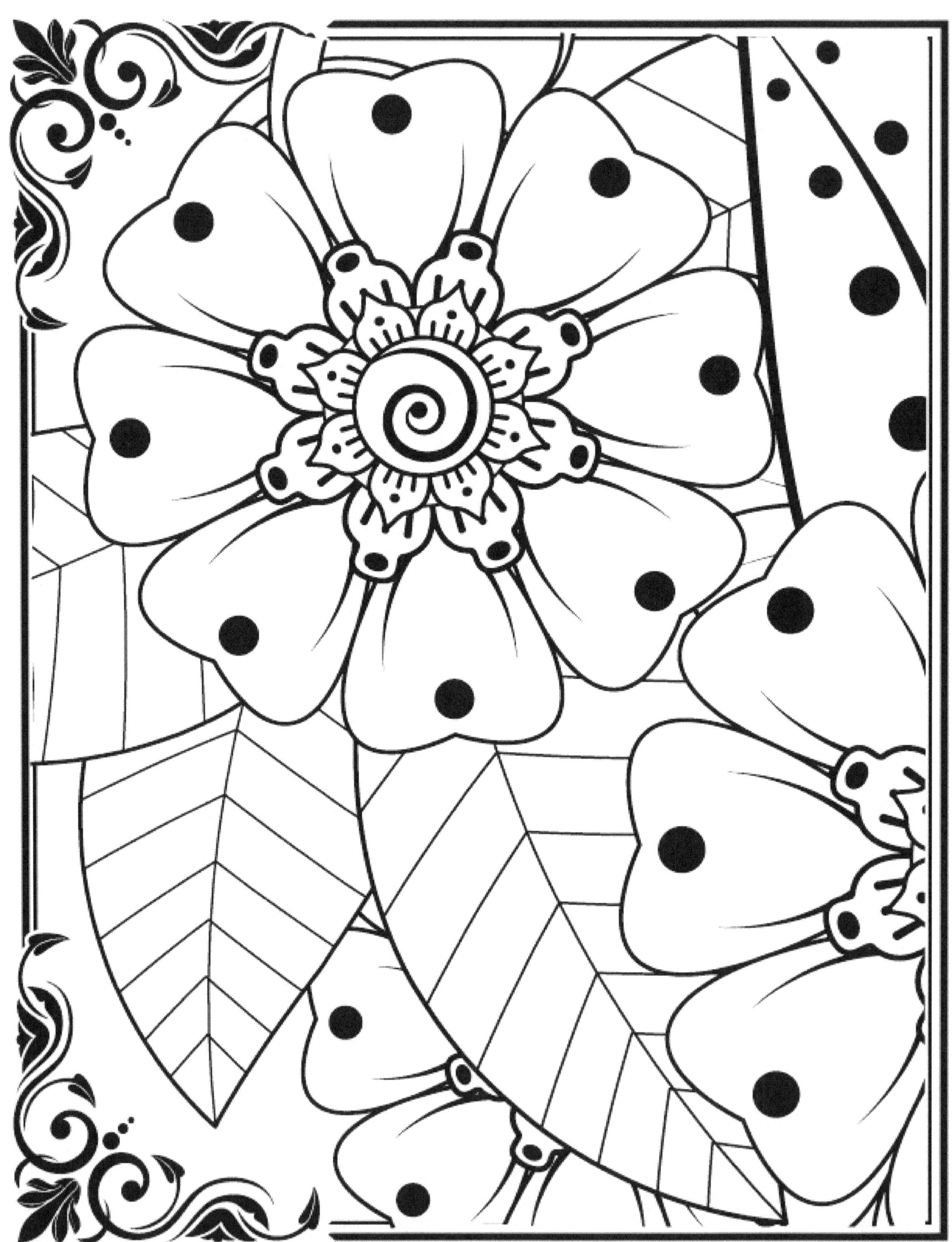

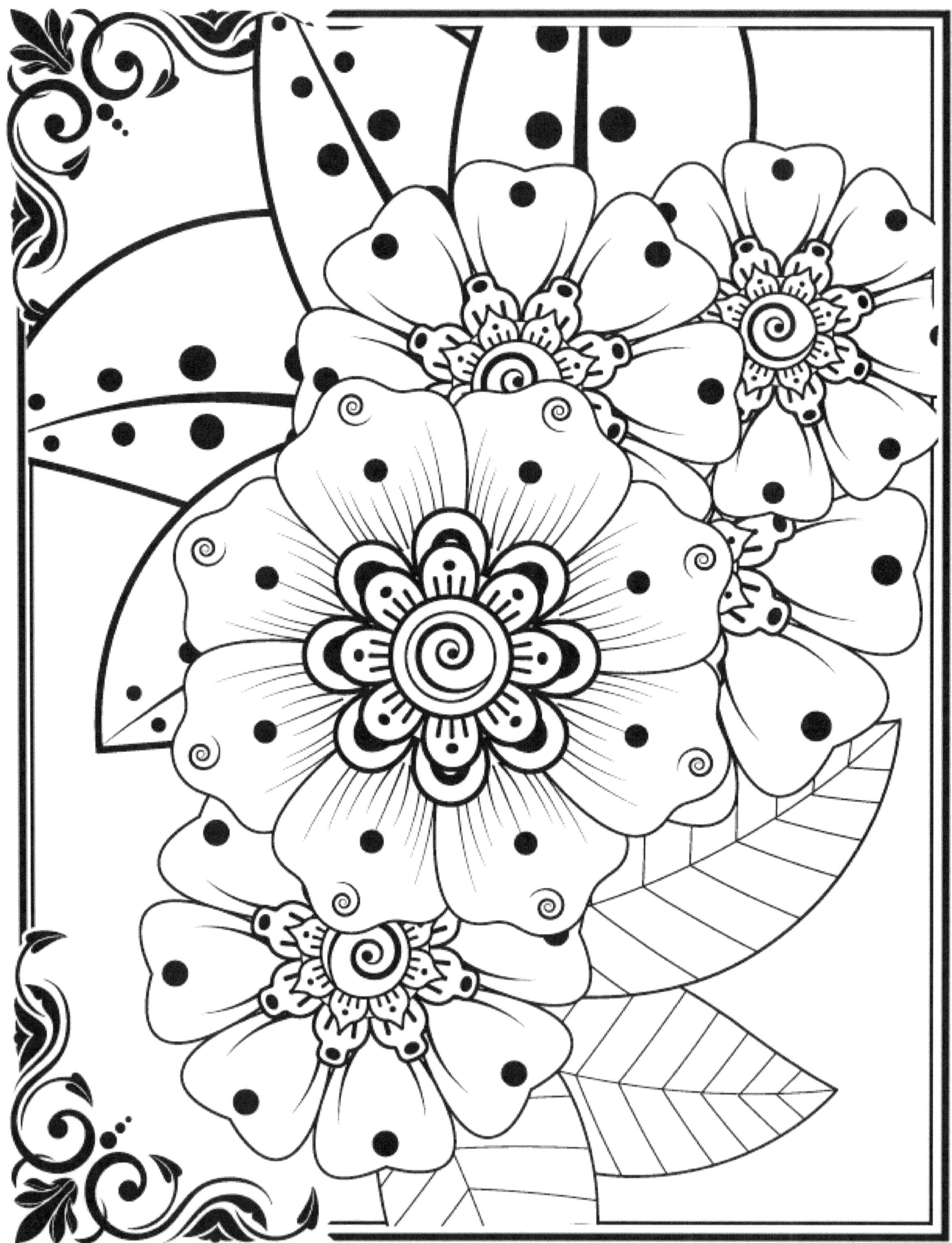

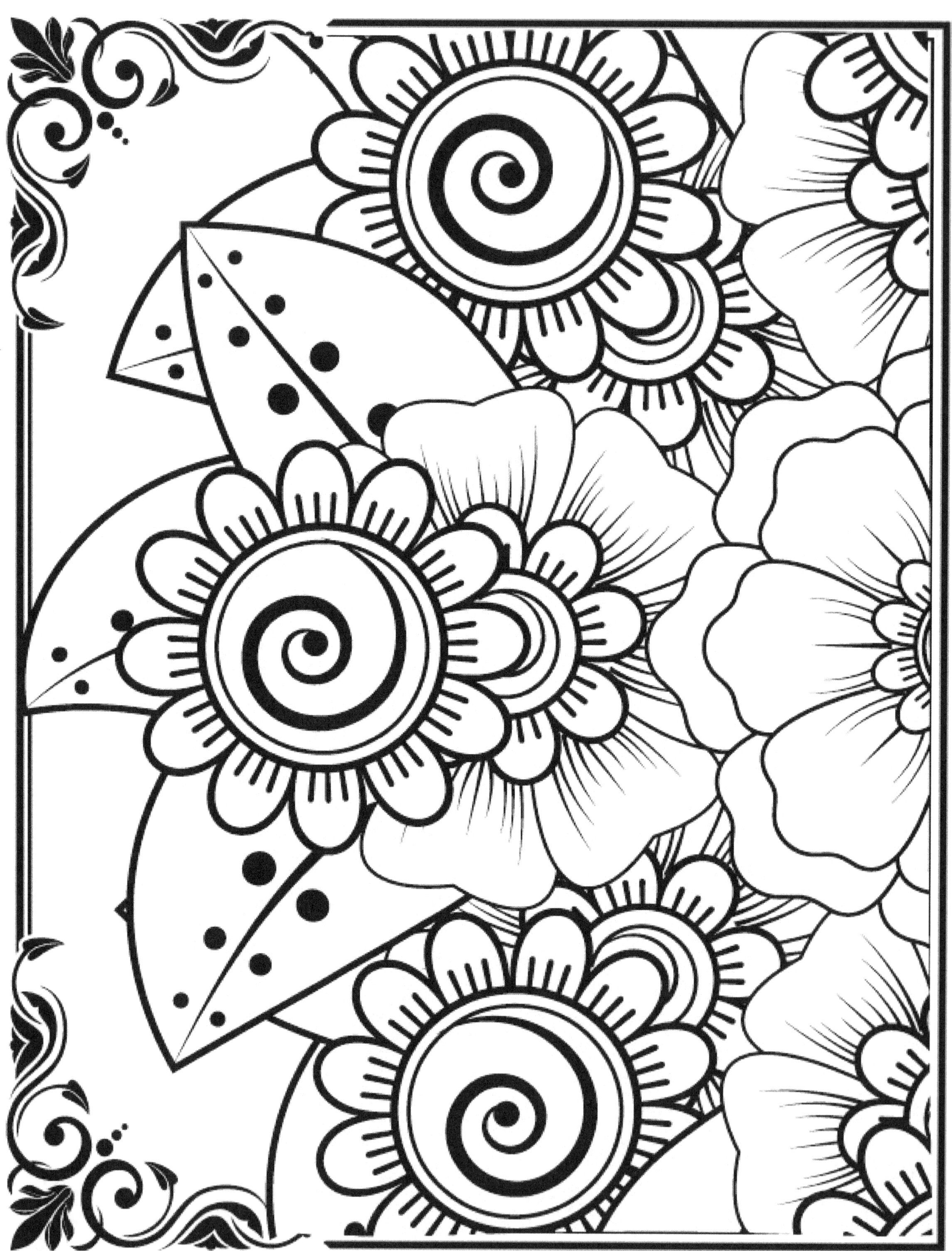

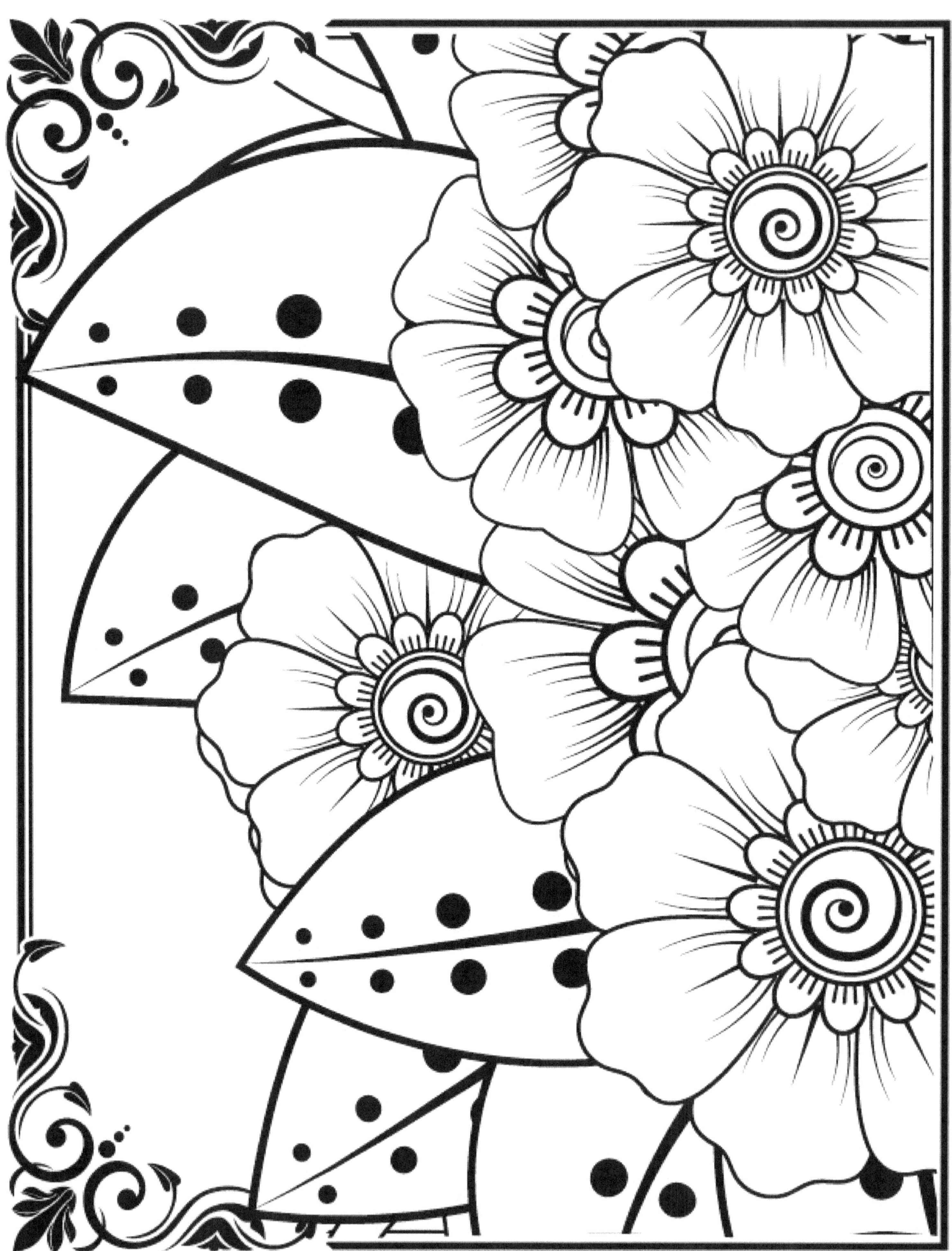

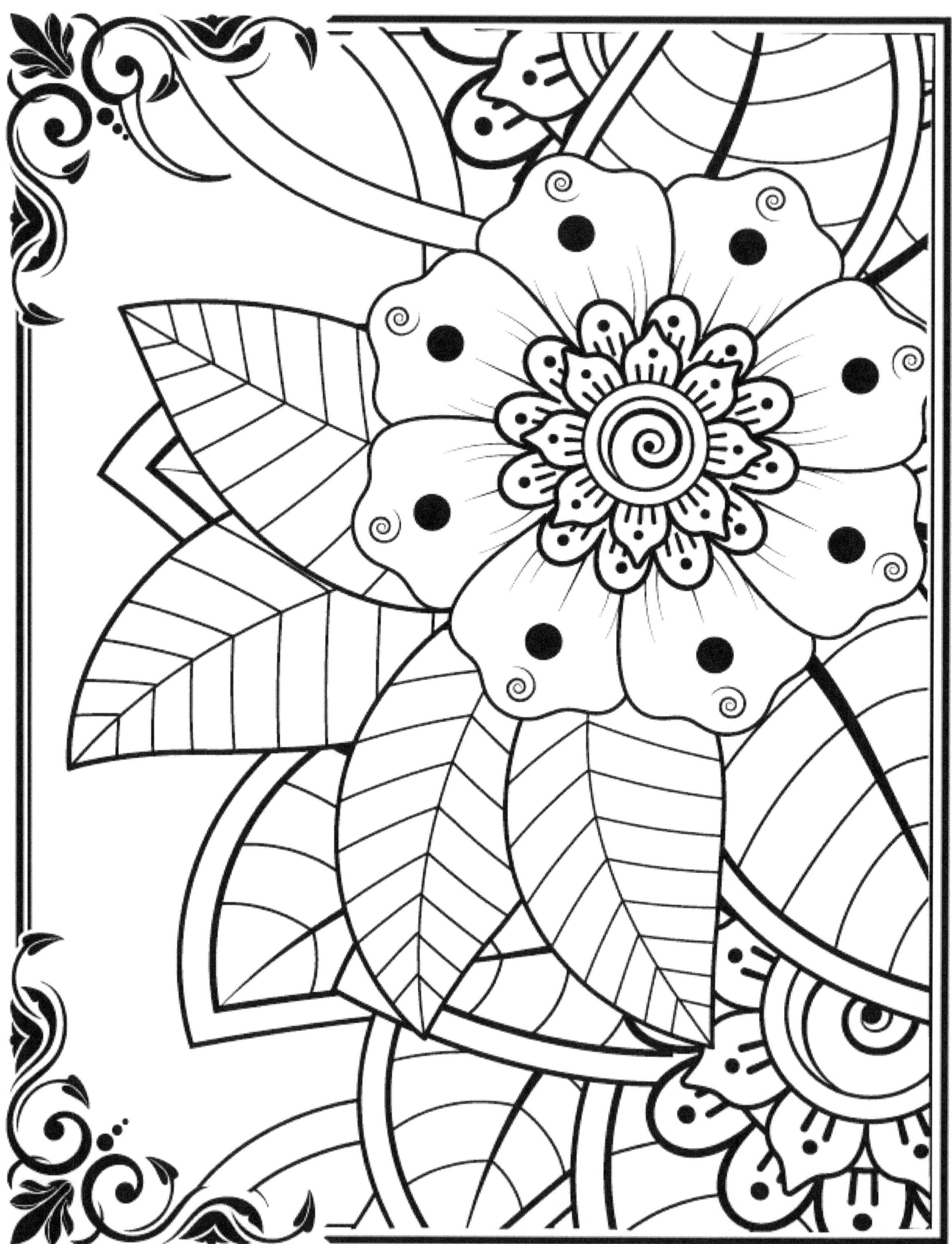

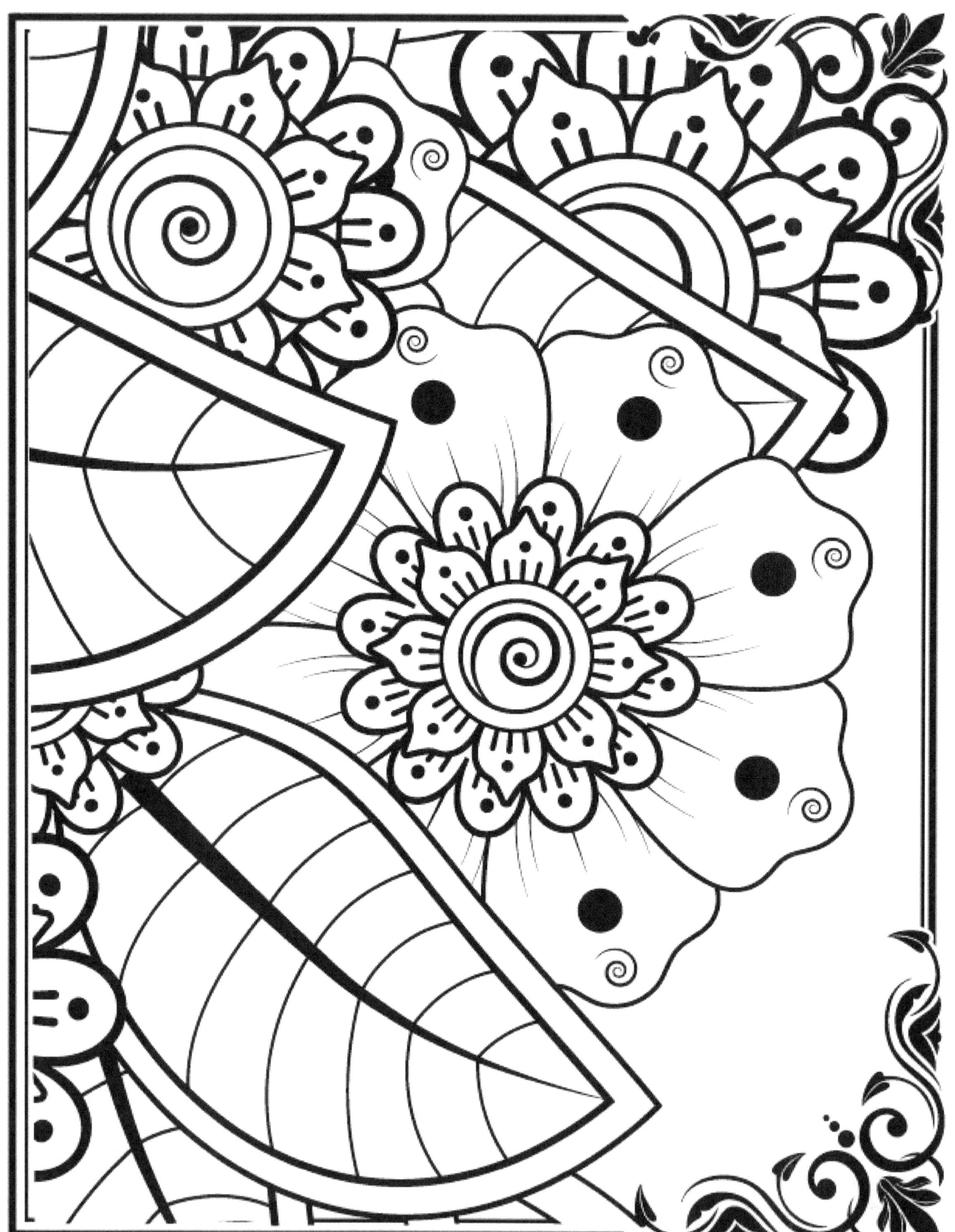

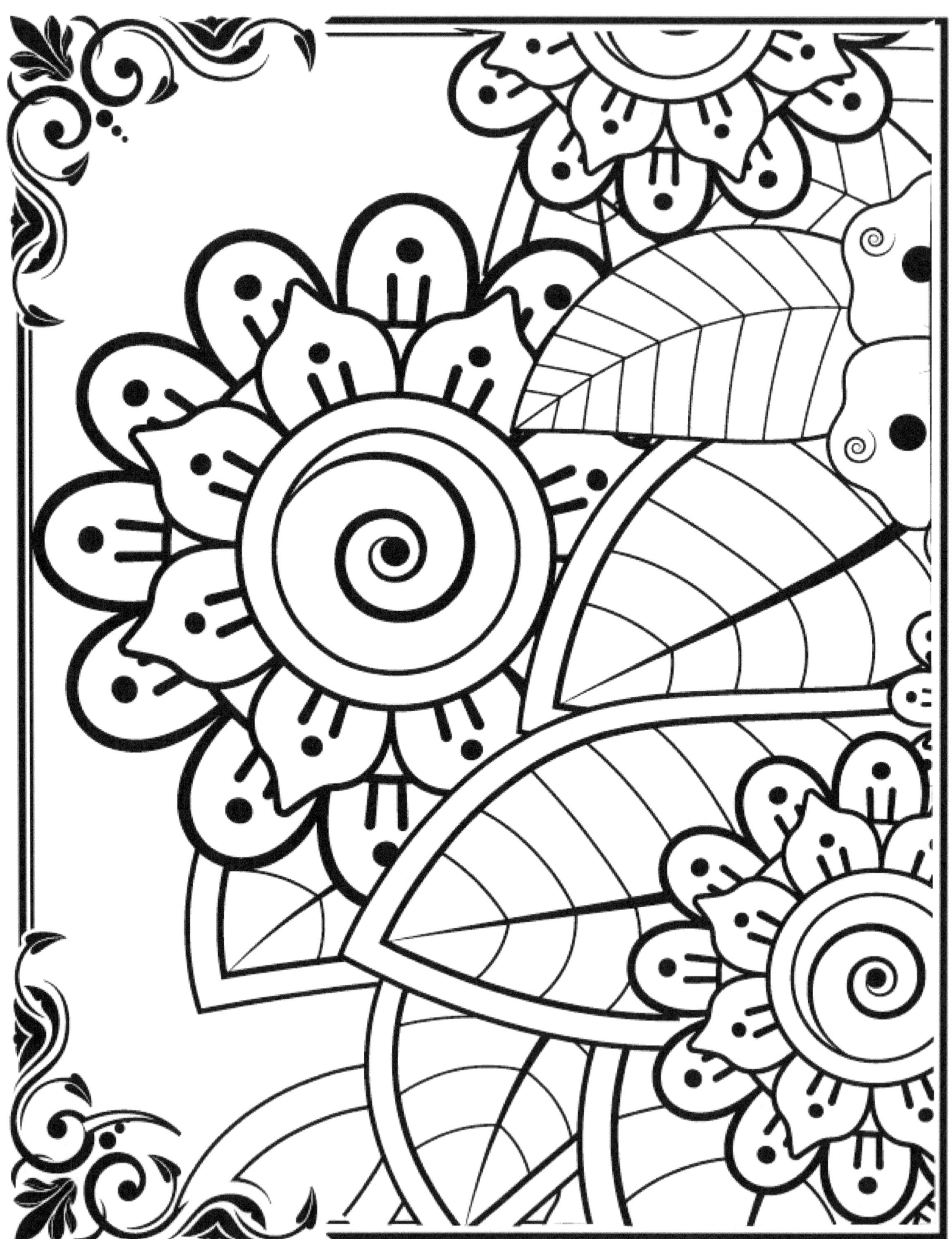

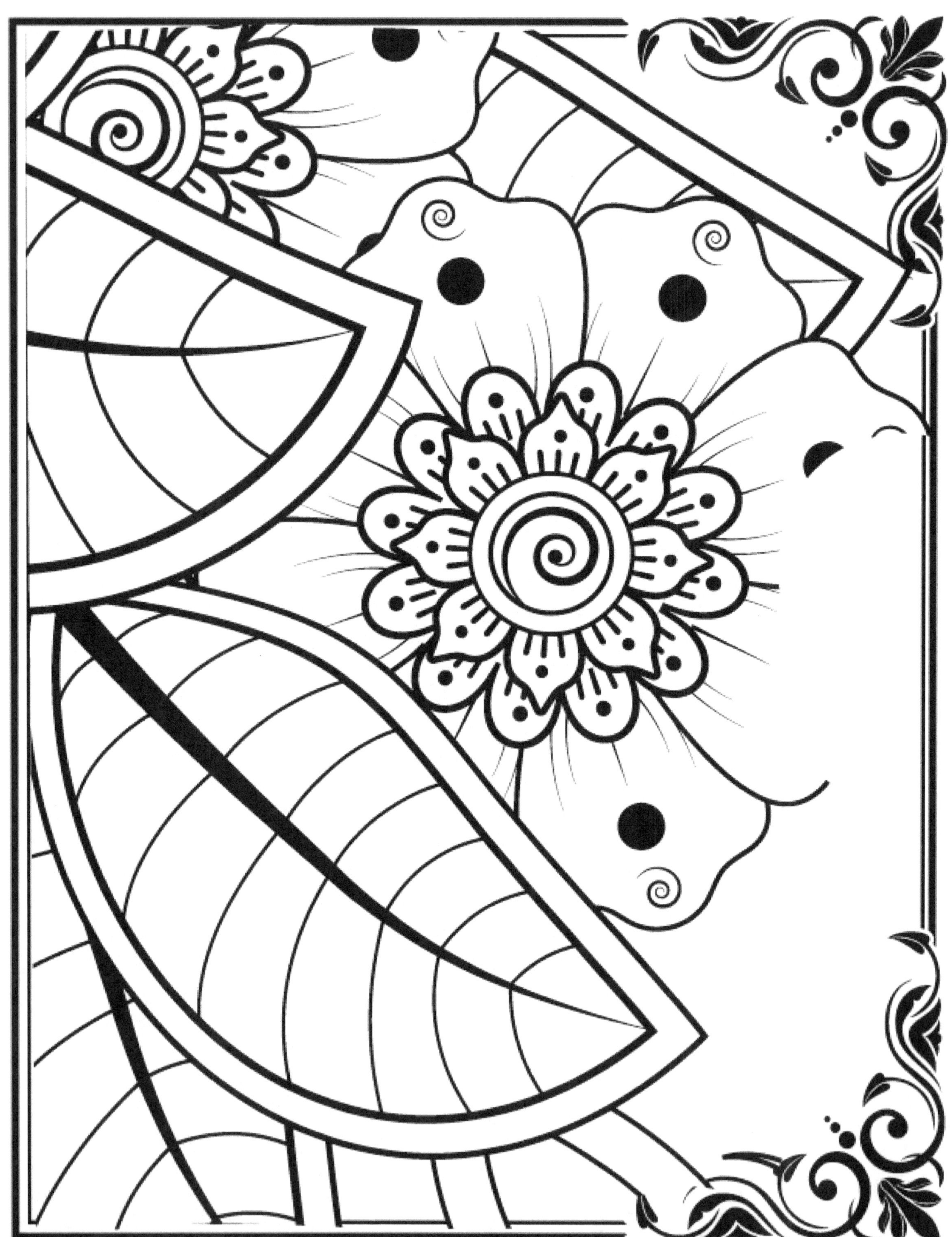

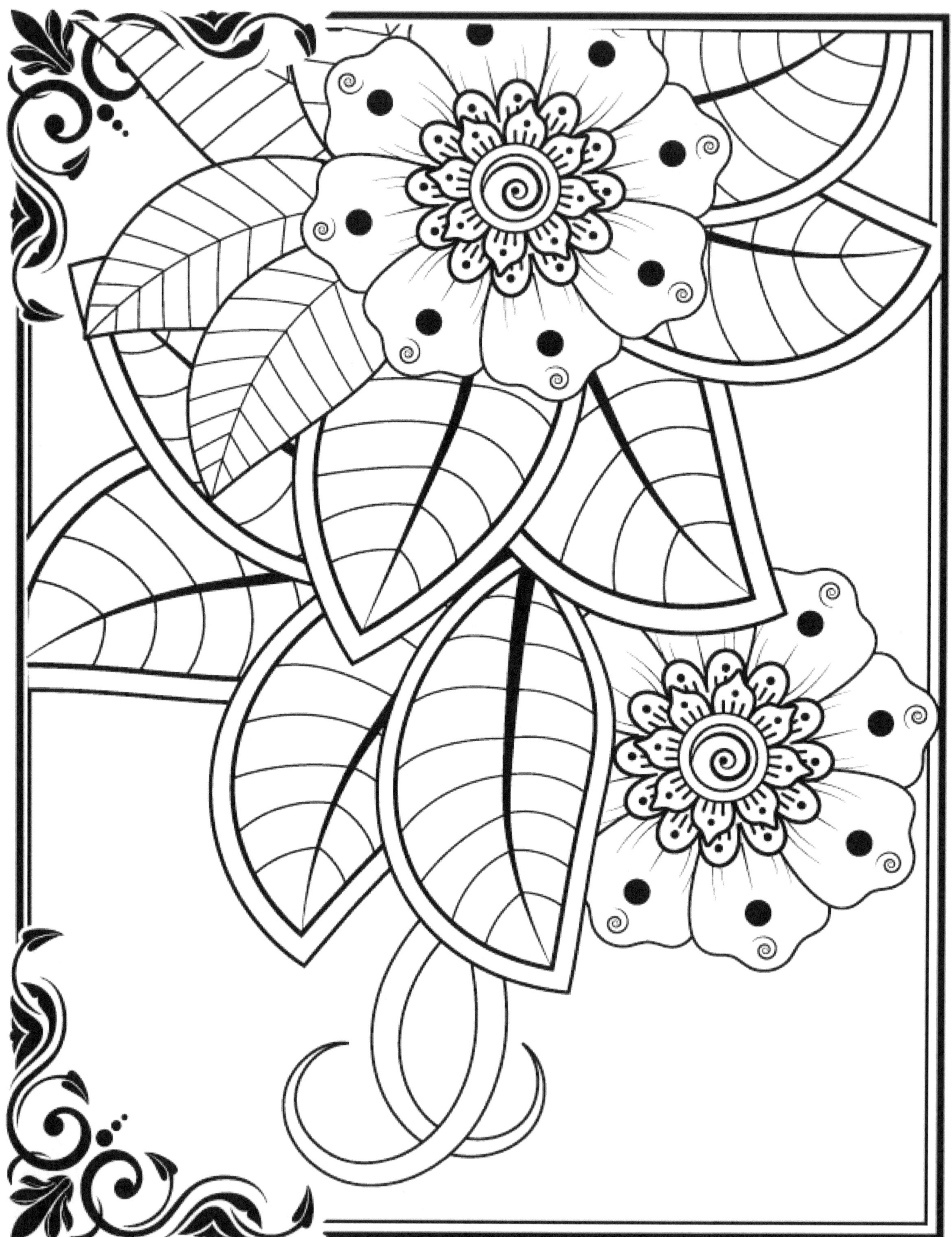

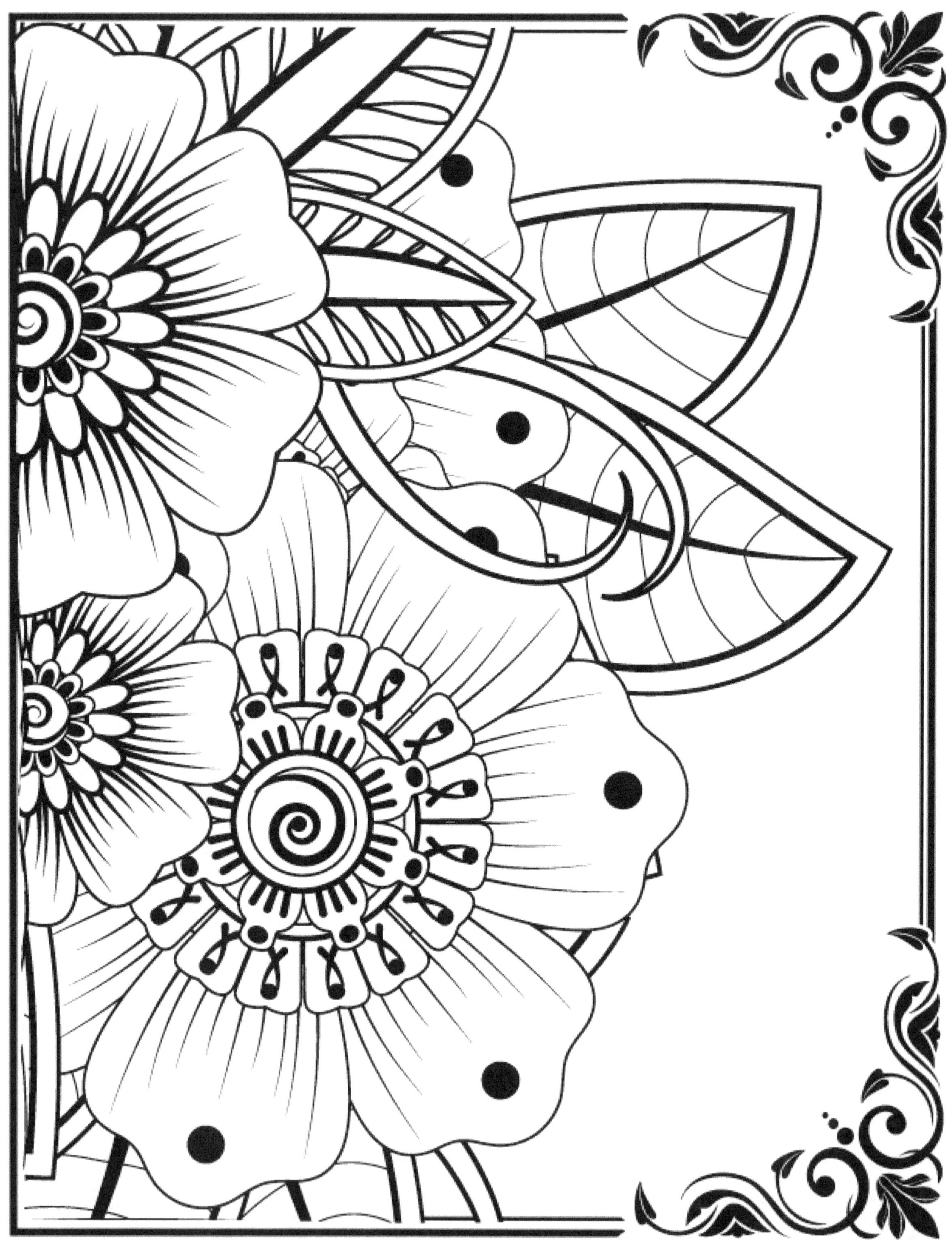

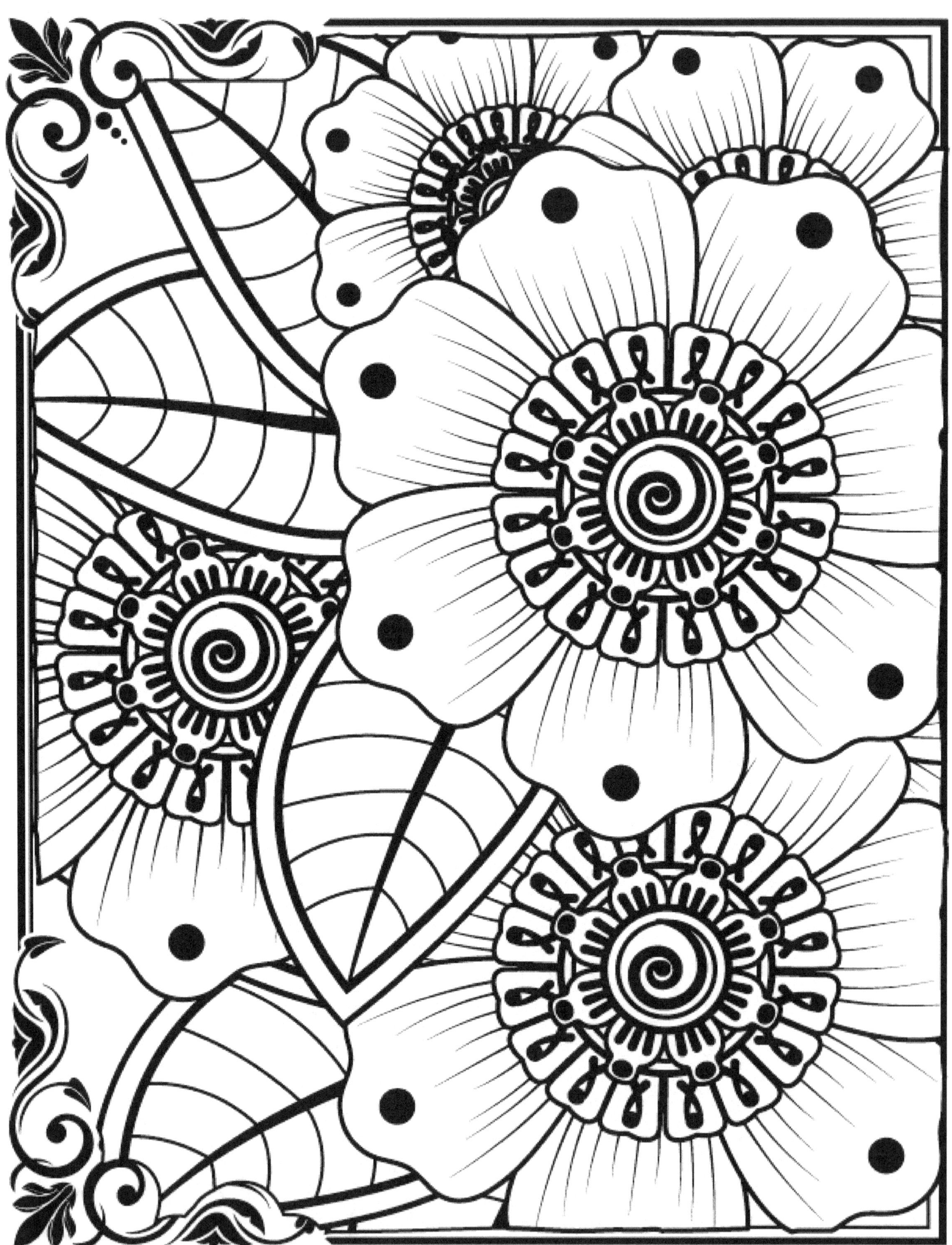

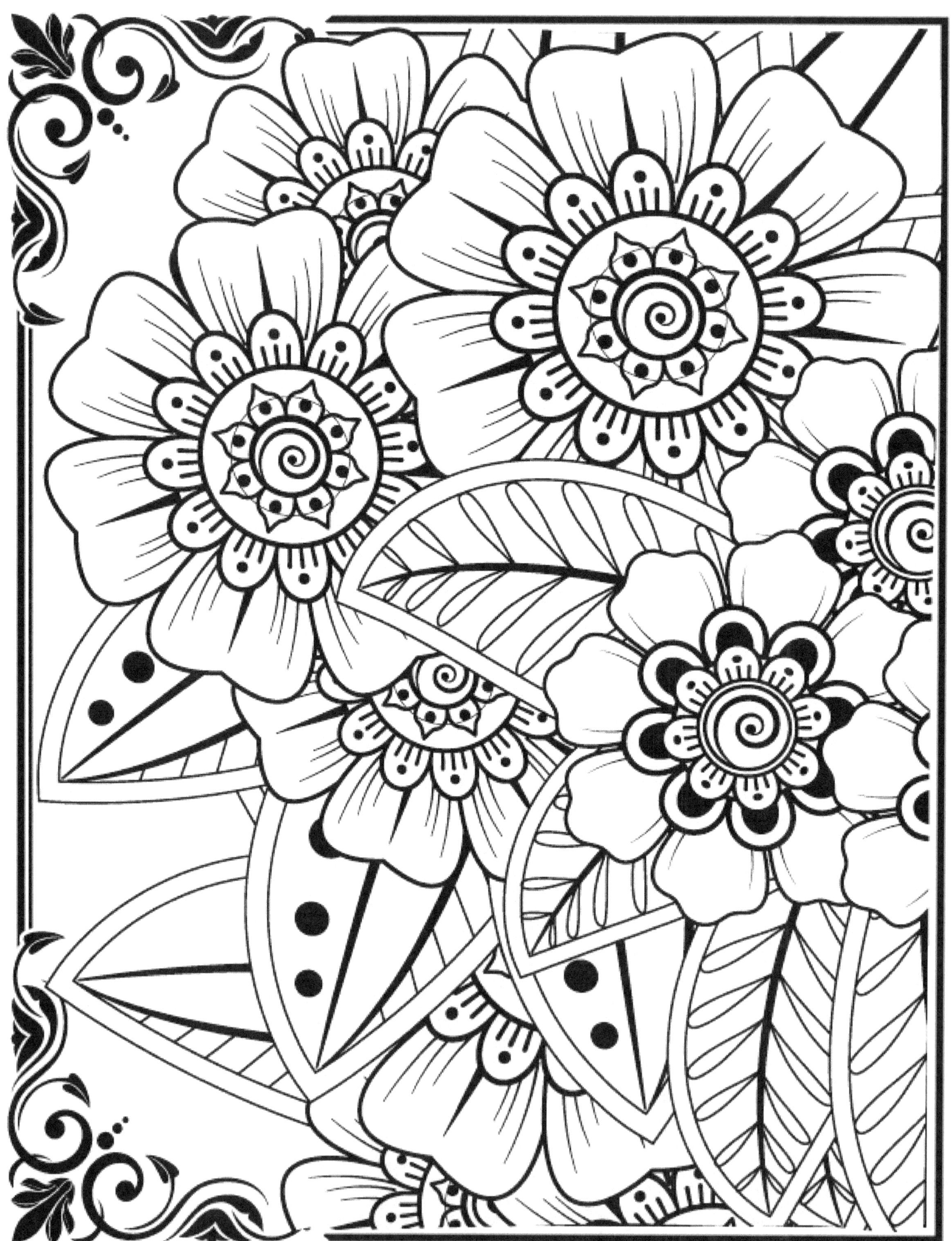

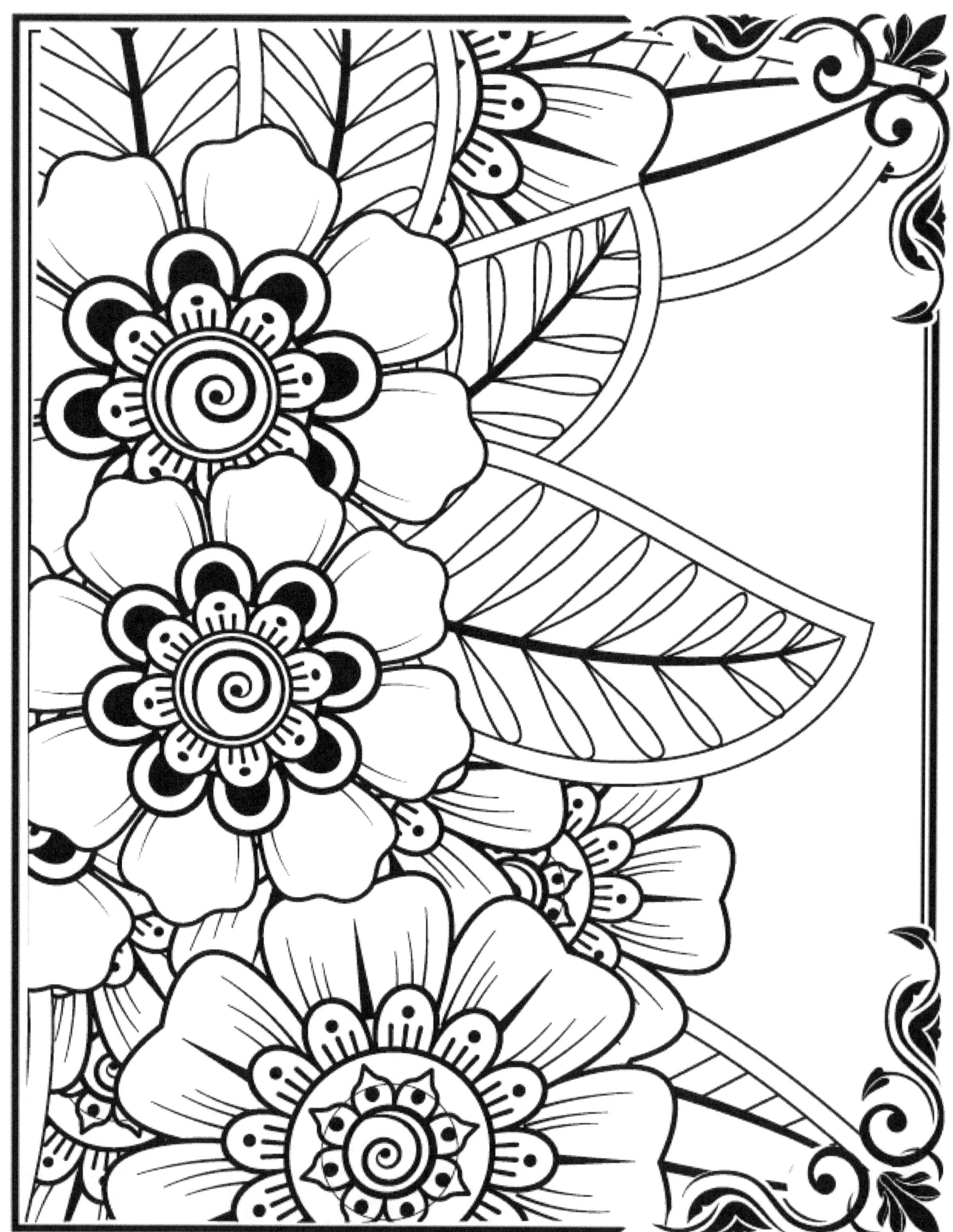

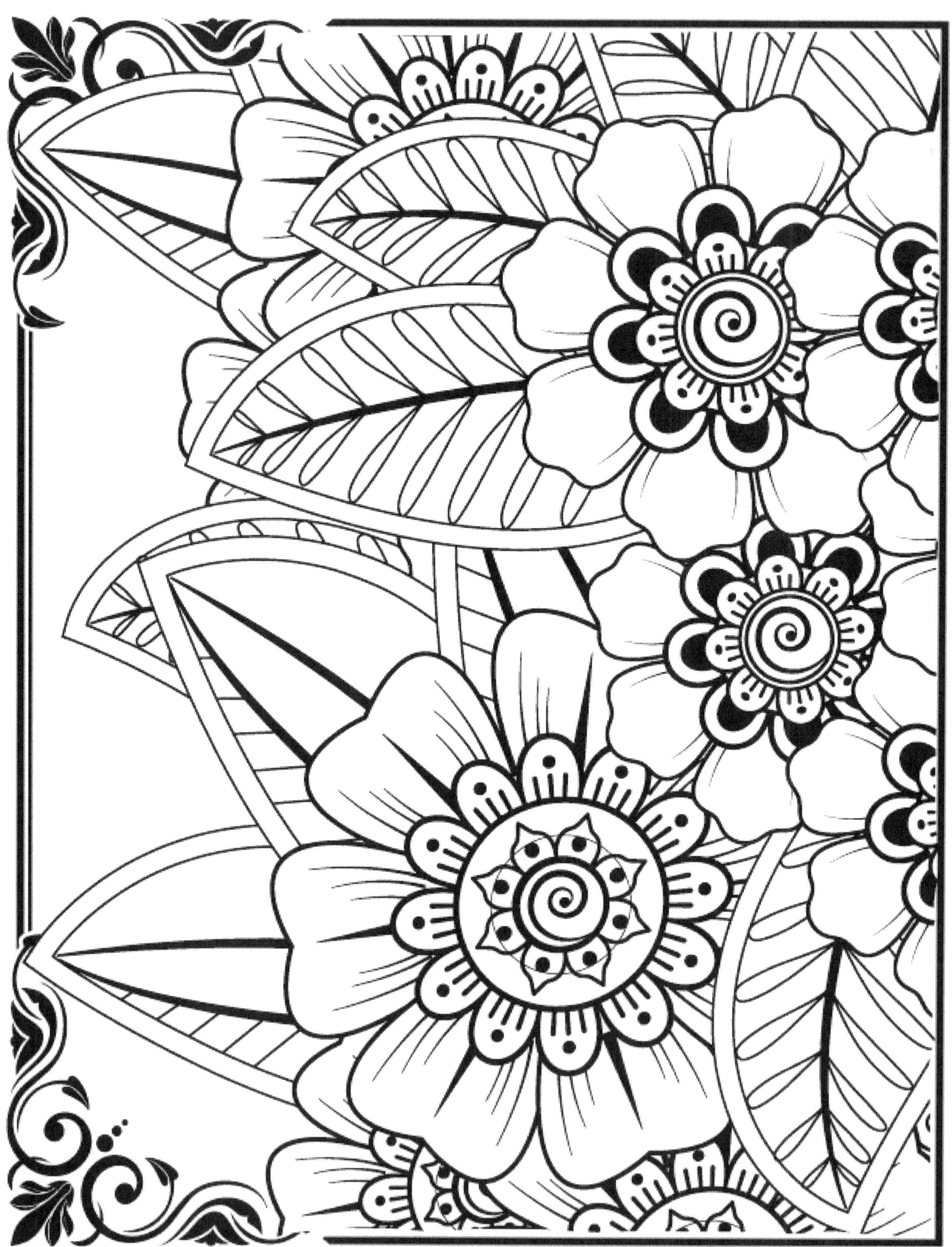

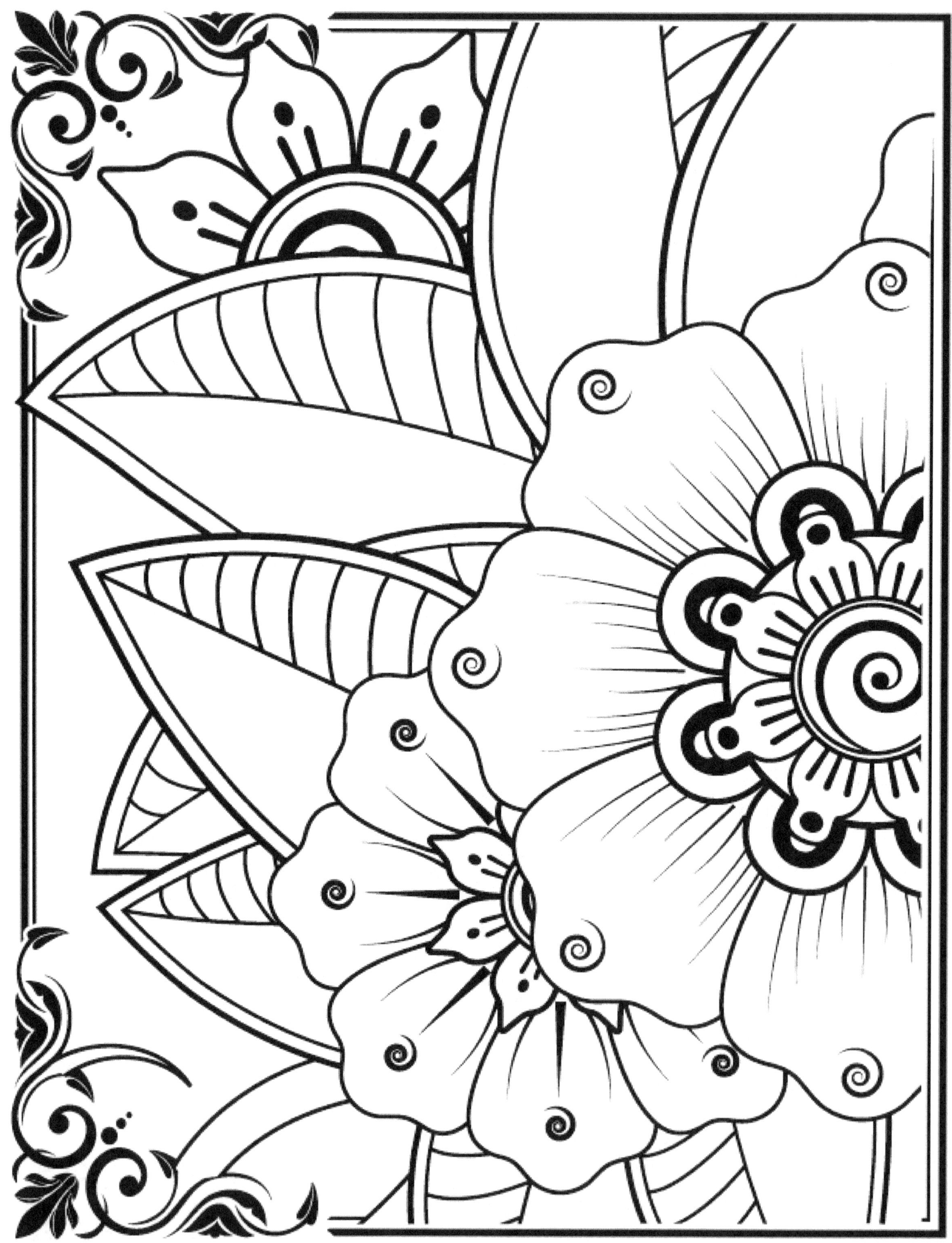

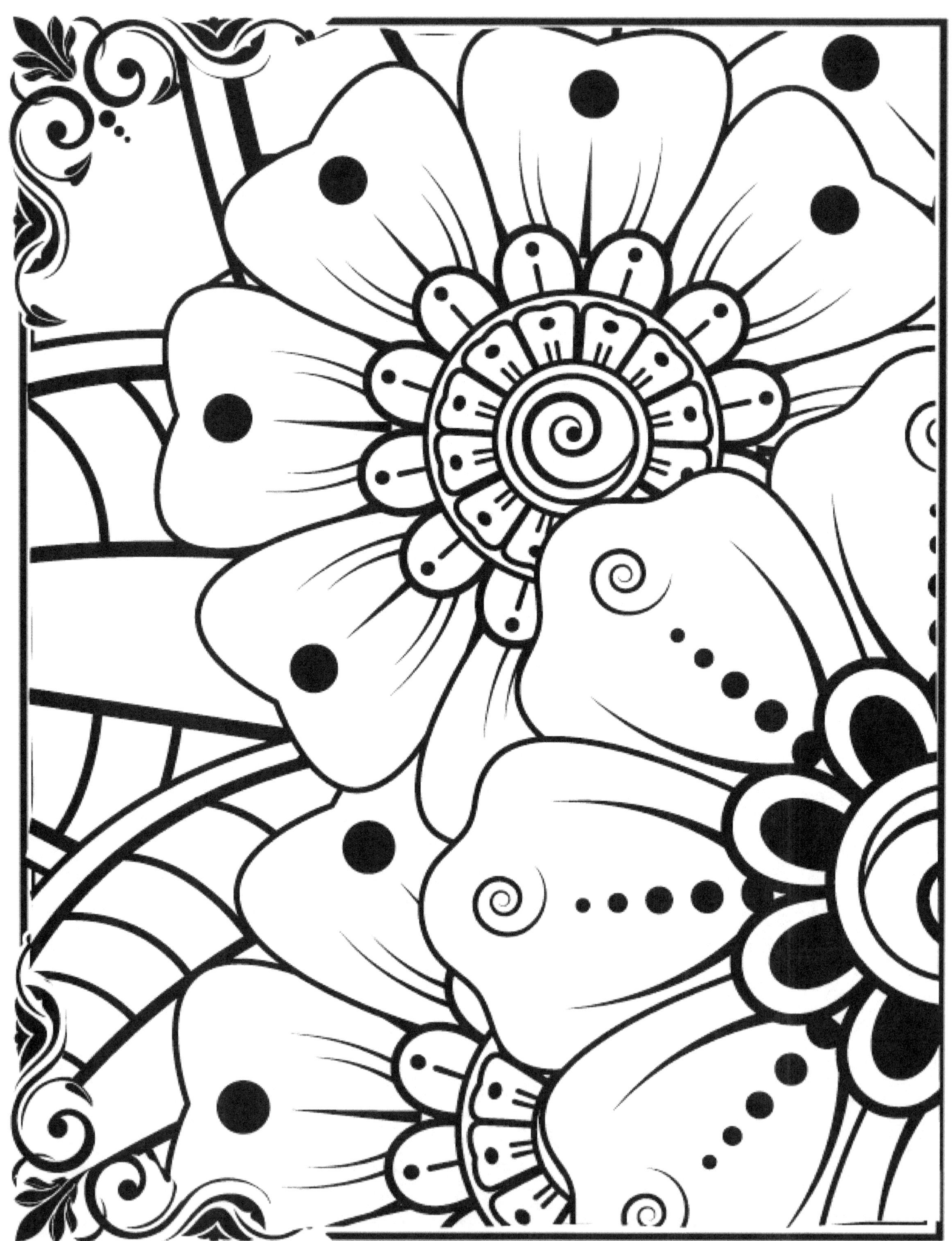

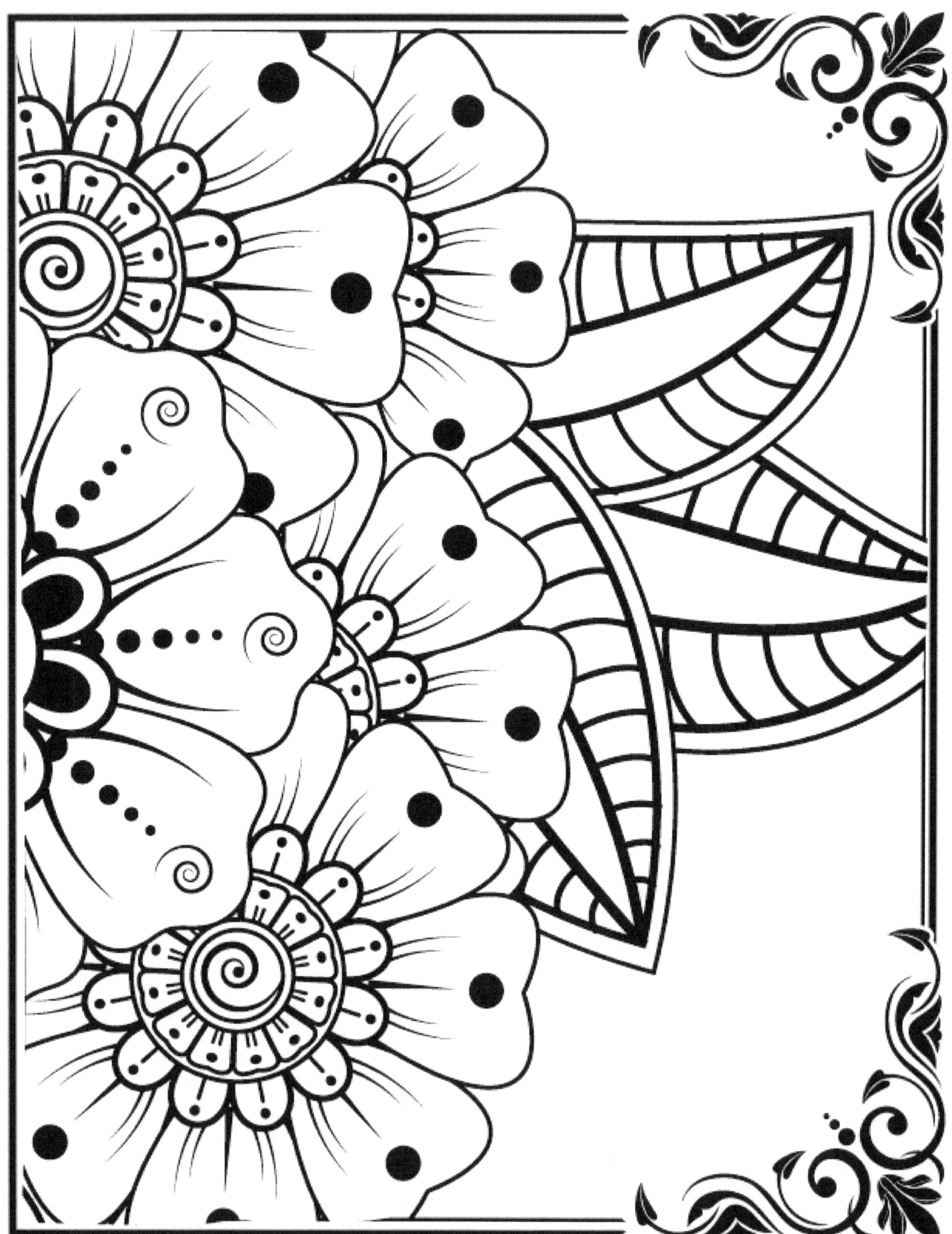

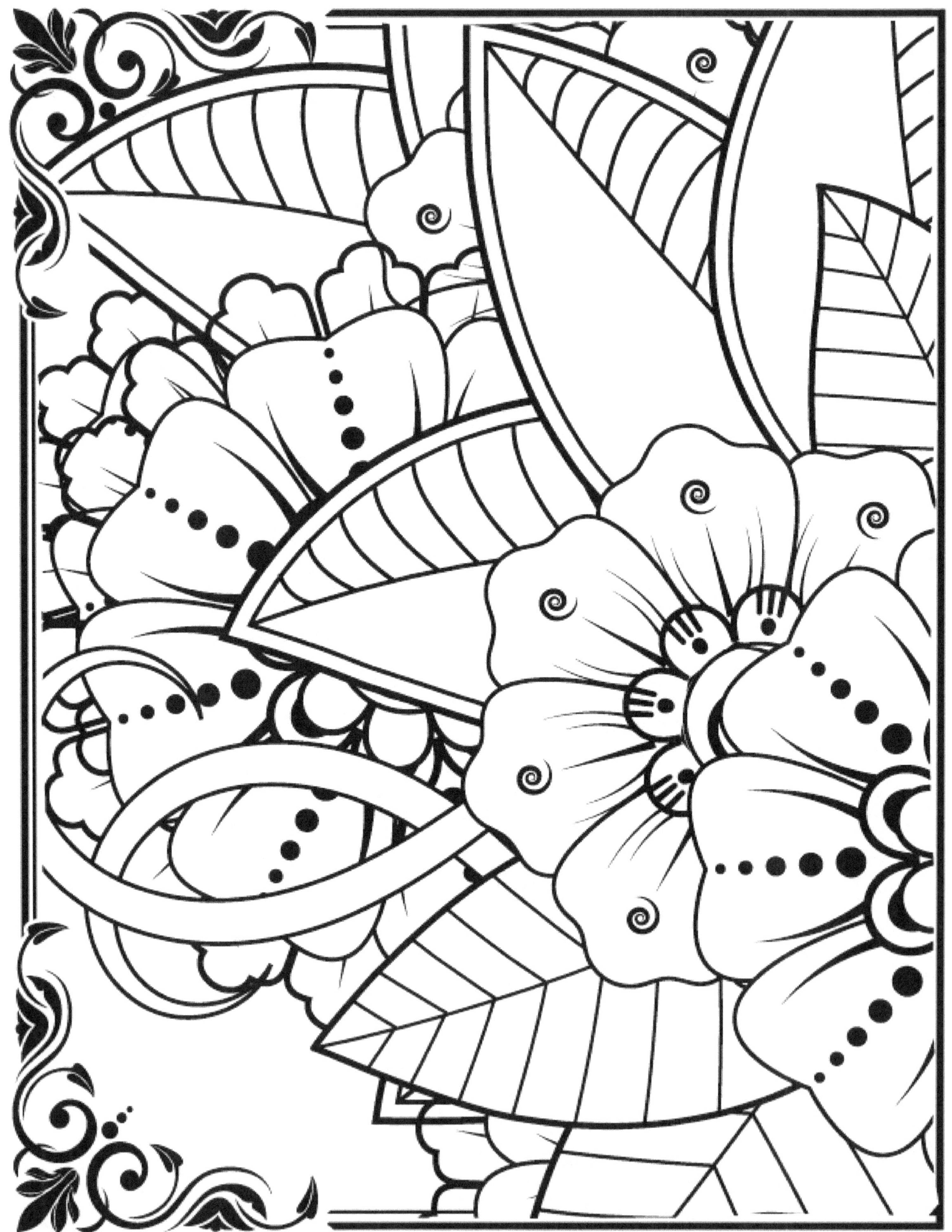

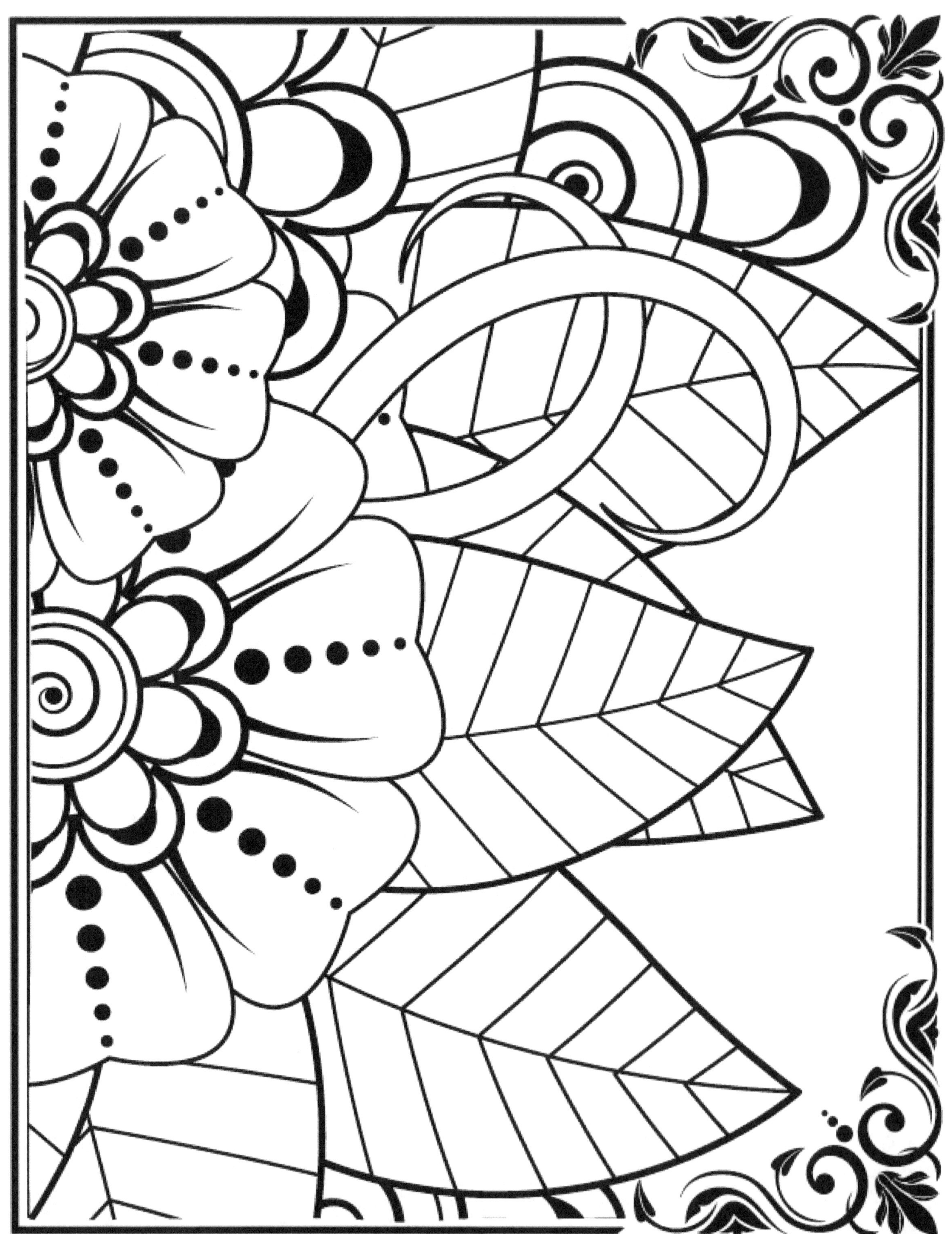

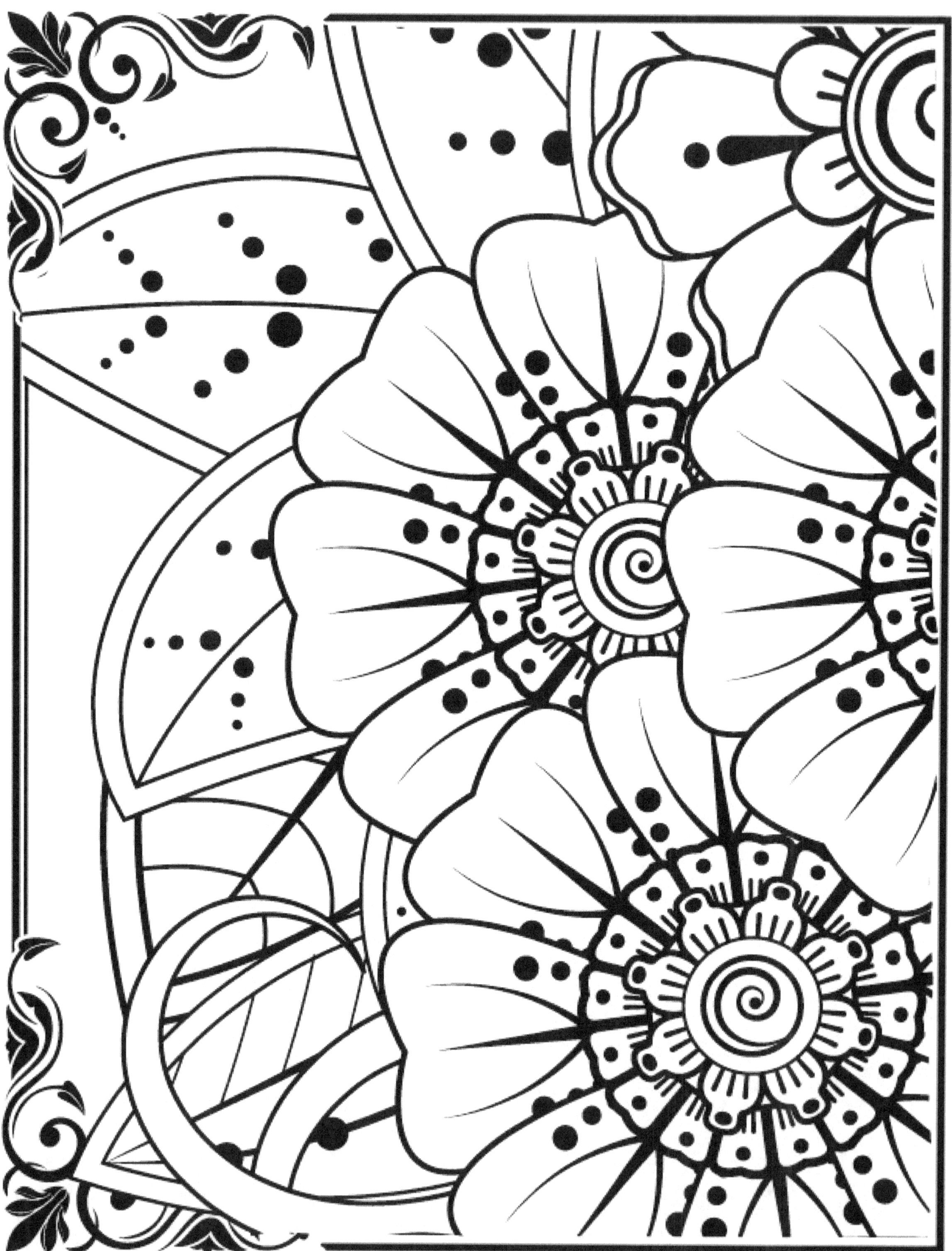

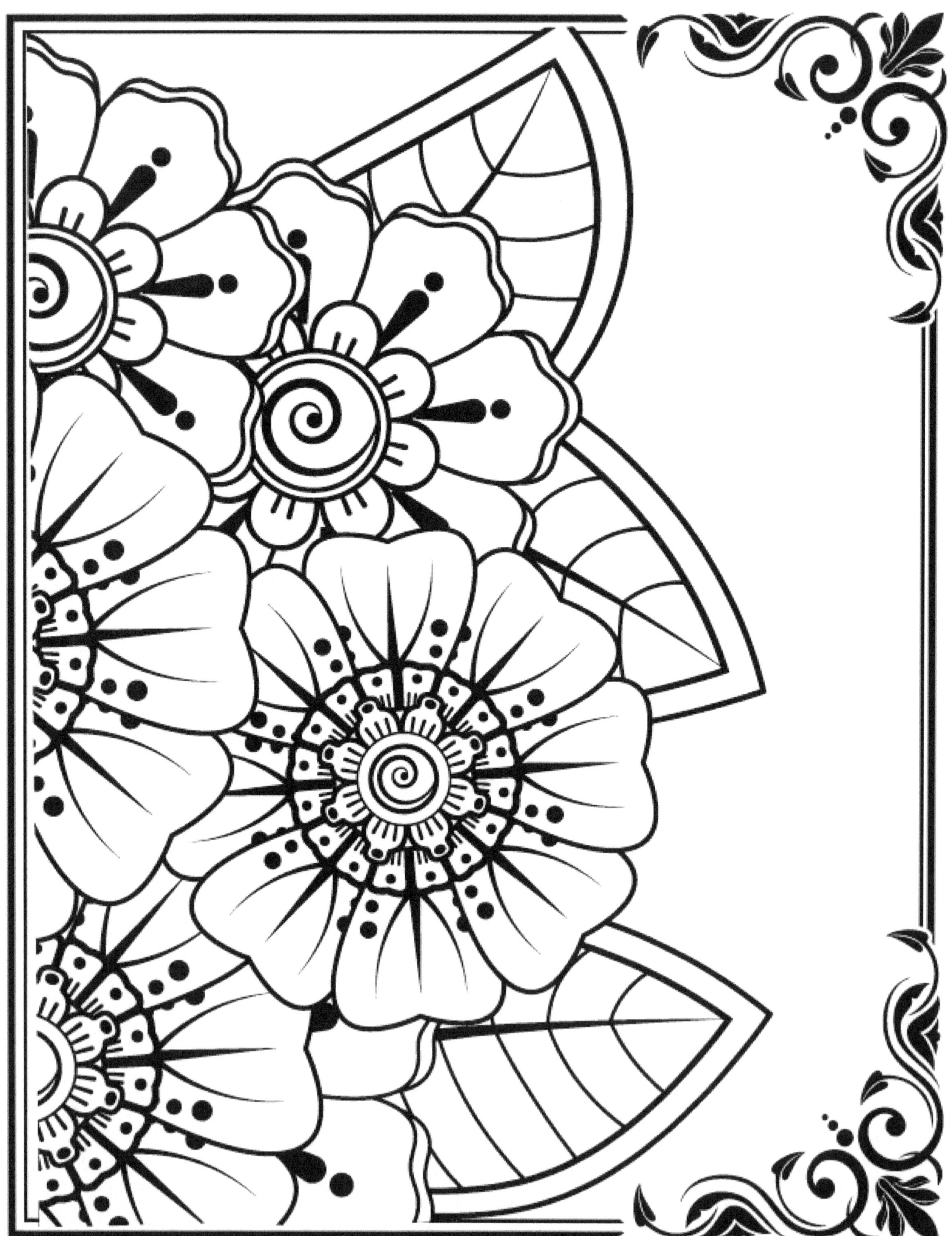

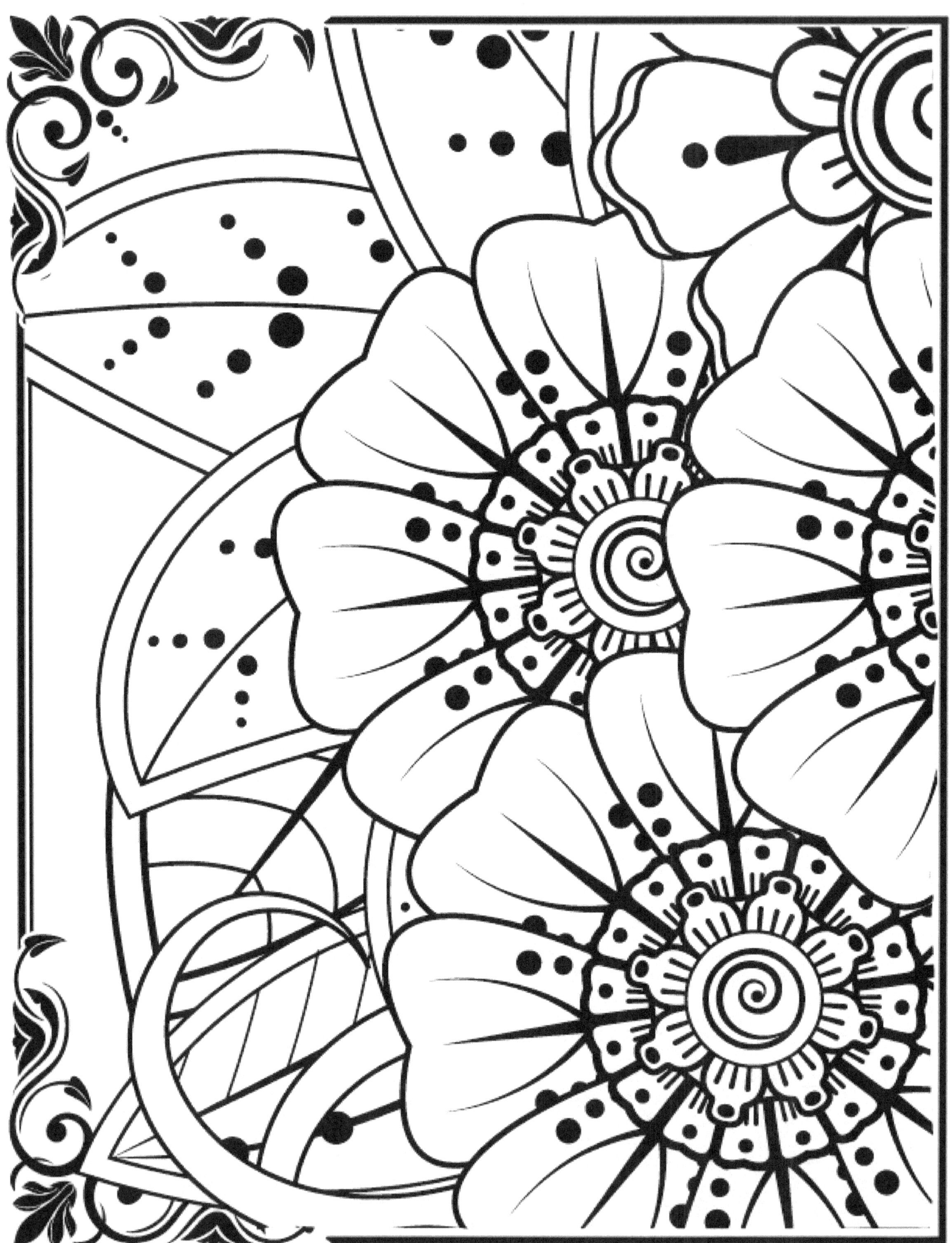